PRENTICE-HALL

Foundations of Economic Geography Series

NORTON GINSBURG, *Editor*

Foundations of Economic Geography Series

A Prologue to Population Geography

WILBUR ZELINSKY

Professor of Geography
The Pennsylvania State University

PRENTICE-HALL, INC., Englewood Cliffs, N.J.

PRENTICE-HALL INTERNATIONAL, INC., *London*
PRENTICE-HALL OF AUSTRALIA, PTY., LTD., *Sydney*
PRENTICE-HALL OF CANADA, LTD., *Toronto*
PRENTICE-HALL OF INDIA (PRIVATE), LTD., *New Delhi*
PRENTICE-HALL OF JAPAN, INC., *Tokyo*

Foundations of Economic Geography Series

Among the various fields of geography, economic geography, perhaps more than any other, has experienced remarkable changes within the past twenty years—so many that it is almost impossible for one scholar to command all aspects of it. The result has been increasing specialization on the one hand and, on the other, a fundamental need for bringing the fruits of that specialization to students of economic geography.

The *Foundations of Economic Geography* Series consists of several volumes, each focusing on a major problem in economic geography. It is designed to bring the student, whether novice or more experienced, to the frontiers of knowledge in economic geography, and in so doing, forcefully to demonstrate the methodological implications of current research —but at a level comprehensible even to those just becoming aware of the fascinating problems in the field as it is developing today.

Each volume stands as a contribution to, understanding in its own right, but the series as a whole is intended to provide a broad cross-section of on-going research in economic geography, stemming from concern with a variety of problems. On the other hand, the series should not be regarded as a complete synthesis of work in economic geography, although the volumes explore in depth certain major issues of keenest interest to economic geographers and others in related fields to a degree impossible in textbooks that attempt to cover the entire field. At the same time, the student is brought face-to-face with the kinds of intellectual

v

and conceptual problems that characterize economic geography in a way that no over-all survey can accomplish. Each volume thus provides a basis for an intensive exploration of issues that constitute the cutting edge of research in this most dynamic and demanding field of knowledge.

As time goes on and new volumes appear in the series, the original volumes will be modified in keeping with new developments and orientations, not only in economic geography, but in the field of geography as a whole. The first volume to appear in the series, Wilbur Zelinsky's *A Prologue to Population Geography*, acts as a bridge between economic and cultural geography and as a means for exploring ideas and methods concerning a problem of increasing interest to geographers and social scientists alike: the growth, diffusion, and distribution of populations throughout the world. Other volumes in the series, whether concerned with trade, retail activities, manufacturing, transportation, or water resources, have similar "bridging" qualities that transcend the narrow limitations of ordinary descriptive handbooks. All are concerned with the new and the fresh, and with the transformation of a traditional field of scholarly interest to one that is highly innovative and pioneering.

NORTON GINSBURG

Contents

toward a typology P**A**RT
of population regions **3**

Maps

ix

The following maps have been adapted from the sources indicated:

Map 1, in part from the *Annals of the Association of American Geographers* (March, 1963), from an article by George Jenks.

Map 2, "Levels of Urbanization," from Norton Ginsburg, *Atlas of Economic Development* (Chicago: The University of Chicago Press, 1961).

Map 3, "Generalized Culture Areas," from Spencer and Johnson, *An Atlas for Anthropology* (Dubuque: William C. Brown Company, 1960).

Map 4, "Socioeconomic Evolution," from *Die Erde*, Vol. 90 (1959), through the courtesy of the author, Professor Hans Bobek, and the publisher, Walter de Gruyter Co.

Map 6, "Levels of Economic Development," from an unpublished map by and through the courtesy of Joseph Schwartzberg.

Map 7, "Generalized Population-Resource Regions," from P. M. Hauser and O. D. Duncan, eds., *The Study of Population* (Chicago: The University of Chicago Press, 1959), and through the courtesy of its creator, Edward A. Ackerman.

Grateful acknowledgment is made for permission to use maps 101HC and 201HC, from the Goode Base Maps Series, Department of Geography, The University of Chicago. Copyright by The University of Chicago.

Introduction

Where do people live, and why do they live there? How many and what sorts of people inhabit different parts of the world? What meanings lie behind these areal patterns? These questions have excited the curiosity of thoughtful persons since the days of Herodotus—probably much earlier. Today, when travel is frequent and so much more is known about the world and its people than ever before, it is only natural that such questions should be repeated more insistently. We must seek the answers not only to appease a casual curiosity, but much more importantly, to help solve critical population problems—and because of the strategic contribution of these answers toward larger scientific questions. If population geography is defined temporarily and rather imperfectly as the science that deals with the spatial aspects of population, then it is not too difficult to show that its exploration can yield facts and ideas of major import both to the demographer—the student of the nature and behavior of populations—and to the geographer—the student of the nature of places.

It is important to make clear the aims of this book. *A Prologue to Population Geography* attempts to explore the nature, uses, and meaning of population geography, its issues, boundaries, and the identity of its major ideas. It is an effort to acquaint the reader with a discipline that may attain practical as well as scientific urgency within a few years. It is designed as a goad to thought and a stimulus to research to be used alongside, but not in place of, other useful substantive and methodological studies. Because this is a work created out of the original chaos of observation and speculation that marks any young science, it has no direct antecedents and no pretensions of permanence or infallibility. The facts and ideas put forward here are based on wide read-

1

ing and a certain amount of research, but much of what follows is still exceedingly tentative in nature.

Part 1 identifies and discusses the nature, subject matter, and boundaries of population geography. Part 2 explores a single population element—the number and areal distribution of people—to illustrate how the discipline explains and interprets the phenomena within its jurisdiction, and how such analysis can yield abundant insight into the general nature of places and society. Part 3 attempts to develop an effective approach to the total geography of the population traits of a region or community.

A rich harvest of facts and ideas has not yet been reaped by the population geographer because this is still the period of germination in the history of his discipline. Although the basic concerns of the field are as old as human history, the indispensable facts and techniques for its study have become available only recently. In fact many alarming shortages in this inventory of data and methods are likely to persist for some time. In addition, the conditions surrounding the emergence of demography as a distinct field within social science and of population studies within the field of geography have not been conducive to their optimal growth.[1] Owing chiefly to its late arrival on the academic scene, demography has never succeeded in winning for itself a secure niche in higher institutions of learning. Many valuable contributions have been forthcoming from the statistical offices of various national and international agencies, a few learned societies, research foundations, and insurance firms; but the great impetus for the growth of demographic theory and analysis has come recently from highly devoted volunteers recruited mainly from the field of sociology, but also from anthropology, economics, political science, history, medical science, ecology, and statistics.

Despite this absence of a firm institutional structure, demography is coming to be recognized as a subject of nearly universal intellectual and practical importance. It draws freely upon the resources of most of the social and biological fields, and in turn, contributes its findings to the enrichment of these studies. The swiftly multiplying population perplexities of the mid-twentieth century argue eloquently for immediate, intensive research in demography. In almost every instance in which a geographic specialty has flourished, its nongeographic counterpart has fared well—for example, the intertwined careers of geology and the geography of landforms, economics and economic geography, or anthropology and cultural geography. Lacking until recently the prod of rapid advance in its companion science, and suffering a dearth of statistics,

---

[1] The history of demography in general is discussed in Frank Lorimer, "The Development of Demography," in Philip M. Hauser and Otis Dudley Duncan, eds., *The Study of Population: An Inventory and Appraisal* (Chicago: Univ. of Chicago, 1959), pp. 124-79. Chapters 7 through 14 in the same work treat the development of the subject in France, Great Britain, Germany, Italy, Brazil, India, the Pacific area, and the United States. The historical background of population geography is analyzed in Glenn T. Trewartha, "The Case for Population Geography," *Annals of the Association of American Geographers,* Vol. 43 (1953), 71-97.

maps, and the endless variety of auxiliary data needed for meaningful analysis, population geography has only now begun to claim serious attention.

The traditional structure of the discipline has also worked against the success of population studies. Geography has customarily been divided into two major segments. The first of these, physical geography, considers the features of an "earth shell" in which the human presence is usually ignored as much as possible. (But man's use of the earth's resources is a major motivation—overtly or implicitly—inspiring much of this "nonhuman" geography.) The other field, human geography, has been concerned with the works of man and a wide variety of human institutions, activities, and ideas. Yet man himself, the key element in almost any geographic equation, whether as the doer of deeds or the user of things, has been neglected by the geographer to a striking degree. Geographers deal primarily with things—objects of considerable size or extent—and secondly, with certain relations and ideas (which would, by definition, exclude population) that generally find some tangible expression in the visible landscape. In recent methodological statements, Trewartha and Hooson have argued persuasively against this issue of visibility, maintaining that population geography constitutes a third primary division of the field, ranking alongside physical and human geography in importance; but this thesis has gained only limited acceptance.[2]

This work affirms that population geography should be a major autonomous branch of the larger field of geography and contends that it has great pragmatic value in being able to enlighten nearly the whole field of geographic and demographic studies, and that population geography is at least as efficient and penetrating as any other strategy in its mode of apprehending the large, complex realities that are the ultimate objectives of the demographer and geographer.

The boundaries between academic disciplines are administrative conveniences, not barricades. Consequently, the student who is nominally a demographer can sometimes perform useful work of a geographic nature, and the geographer may occasionally find himself toiling by the demographer's side. It is useful to note, however, that the two fields diverge in their basic aims, though they share a common interest in the territorial distribution of population. The demographer is ultimately concerned with the intrinsic nature, the universal attributes, of populations, with the systematic principles governing their composition, socioeconomic correlates, behavior, and changes; the spatial dimension is incidental to this central purpose.

Even though there is a need for a comprehensive treatise on population geography that would provide reasonably thorough systematic treatment of each important topic within the field and analysis of the

    [2] Trewartha, "The Case for Population Geography," and David J. M. Hooson, "The Distribution of Population as the Essential Geographical Expression," *Canadian Geographer*, No. 17 (1960), 10-20.

population content of each inhabited region of the world, much pre-liminary work must be done before an adequate monograph can be undertaken. Data are just now appearing for many areas that were notably deficient in reliable demographic facts, but serious regional gaps still persist. For too many countries, the quality and variety of data leave a great deal to be desired; few territories have adequate maps, and even fewer have detailed geographical analyses of population.

The most serious shortage is in methodology. The guiding principles for the organization of research and the marshaling of facts and ideas have been nebulous at best. This work attempts to construct a frame-work for the discipline: It endeavors to outline, structure, and give gen-eral procedures of population geography, and to state some of the central questions it is seeking to illuminate as well as some of the more likely approaches to these questions. In no sense can this be regarded as the *précis* for the larger work yet to be written; it is only a kind of introductory chapter. Even though many isolated facts and regional examples are briefly quoted, there is no full-scale effort to apply the proposed techniques to the analysis of any topic or area.

Some previous knowledge of the elements of geography is assumed, but not enough to deter the interested nongeographer. Although the volume is addressed primarily to geographers of all levels, including those only incidentally concerned with population studies as well as those seriously considering active work within this field, the hope is that it will also prove useful to many others as an introduction to a subject of wide intellectual appeal.

PART 1 *what does the population geographer study?*

CHAPTER ONE

The substance and limits of population geography

The Field Defined

Population geography can be defined accurately as the science that deals with the ways in which the geographic character of places is formed by, and in turn reacts upon, a set of population phenomena that vary within it through both space and time as they follow their own behavioral laws, interacting one with another and with numerous non-demographic phenomena.[1] "Place" in this context may be a territory of any extent, from a few acres up to the entire surface of the earth. In briefer terms, the population geographer studies the spatial aspects of population in the context of the aggregate nature of places.

The essential purpose of this field is far broader and deeper than the elementary task of stating where how many of what sort of people reside. As in all other branches of geography, the simple "where" of things cannot be accepted as a sufficient definition of the scope and purpose of population geography. "Geographic" is not a synonym for "locational." To be analytical, geography must look for the interrelatedness of things that vary through space. It must probe the generally complicated flux of cause and effect among these interrelated features that endow specific places with unique personalities.

We find, then, that the population geographer is concerned with three distinct and ascending levels of discourse: (1) the simple description of the location of population numbers and characteristics; (2) the explanation of the spatial configurations of these numbers and character-

---

[1] The same definition would suffice for almost any other systematic division of geography with suitable substitutions for the terms "population" and "nondemographic."

istics; and (3) the *geographic* analysis of population phenomena (the interrelations among areal differences in population with those in all or certain other elements within the geographic study area).

Ideally, the geographer would look to the cartographer for maps showing the location of population features, and to the demographer for adequate accounts of their genesis. Meanwhile, the geographer's attention could be concentrated on the strictly geographic task of interpreting the role of the population element within the universe of geographic fact. But such is seldom the case. All too often the population geographer must expend a disproportionate amount of energy on the elementary chore of fabricating usable population maps where none are otherwise available; and much of his remaining time must be spent in searching for the immediate factors that mold the patterns appearing on the maps, thus leaving scant opportunity for the more complex process of true geographic analysis. There is some compensation, however, in the extensive overlapping of the three functions: It is difficult for the geographer to map population features without formulating some hypotheses about their origin; and any inquiry into these origins will inevitably approach a geographic level as it reaches further into the web of influences surrounding most demographic conditions.

The Cartographic Representation of Population Data

Which demographic phenomena does the geographer map, explain, and interpret? First and obviously, the absolute number of individuals. Like other demographic material, this information usually comes to the geographer in tabular form; but it must be translated into cartographic terms prior to geographical exploitation. Verbal paraphrases of the location of people can often help, but the map is the one indispensable tool in population geography, not only for numbers, but also for other demographic phenomena. Since map portrayal of such phenomena is a problem closely resembling the ones found in mapping other kinds of statistics, the technicalities in question need not be examined here.[2] There are, nonetheless, a few special annoyances in population mapping that must be pointed out. Greatly accentuated by rapid urban growth in recent decades, areal disparity in the distribution of people poses an acute dilemma for the draftsman trying to depict absolute numbers with intelligible symbols. There may be no satisfactory solution, though many attempts have been made. As an alternative to showing absolute values, the cartographer often elects the "density" map. In this medium, symbols

[2] For useful discussions of the theory and practice of population mapping—and statistical mapping in general—consult: F. J. Monkhouse and H. R. Wilkinson, "Population Maps and Diagrams," in *Maps and Diagrams* (London: Methuen, 1952), pp. 217-80; Otis Dudley Duncan, "The Measurement of Population Distribution," *Population Studies*, XI (1957), 27-45; and chaps. 8 and 9 in Arthur H. Robinson, *Elements of Cartography*, 2nd ed. (New York: Wiley, 1960), pp. 136-77.

indicate the average number of residents per unit area within a parcel whose boundaries are set by the rules of the particular kind of density map involved. It is quite easy, but fallacious, to assume that the values so represented are an index to population "pressure." Because there is no way of telling what proportion of land is occupied, how it is used, or what the economic properties of the land might be from the map alone, the density map does not in any sense denote a functional relationship between man and territory. It is simply a quantitative statement, in visual form, of the location of population. Some of the several techniques commonly used for showing absolute numbers and population density are illustrated in Map 1.

The most trying problems faced by the population mapper are inherent in the nature of human populations: the rapidity with which numbers and characteristics can and often do change; and the impossibility of locating people precisely, even when census data approach the ideal in quality. In most populations an appreciable number of individuals migrate, and many more oscillate daily, weekly, or seasonally between places of work and residence or between two or more residences. The expression of these dynamic facts through the relatively static medium of the map is an almost insurmountable task.

The Topical Limits of Population Geography

If we define "population" in the broadest terms, then the range of topics treated by the demographer and the population geographer includes anything pertaining to human beings and the social sciences. Such a mass of social, economic, psychological, cultural, and political detail would obviously exceed the grasp of any single group of specialists. Thus it is necessary to circumscribe fairly sharply the field of population studies.

For practical purposes, we may equate the resulting list of human characteristics with those appearing in the census enumeration schedules and vital registration systems of the more statistically advanced nations. These, in turn, are such facts as can be quickly and reliably collected from individual respondents by enumerators or registrars with only a moderate amount of training. For the most part, then, the demographic characteristics are those readily perceptible in individuals or families, while other equally important characteristics, detectable only by skillful or protracted observation of the larger group or by intensive study of individuals, lie beyond the limits of population geography and are largely the cultural geographer's responsibility. This line between the population geographer and the cultural geographer is a convenient, but highly arbitrary, permeable affair.[3] Nondemographic social and

---

[3] Deciding the names and content of some of the various subdivisions of human geography, particularly those of a noneconomic nature, and the placement of their common boundaries is a major problem. "Human geography," as the term for the study covering all aspects of the geography of human beings, appears to be generally

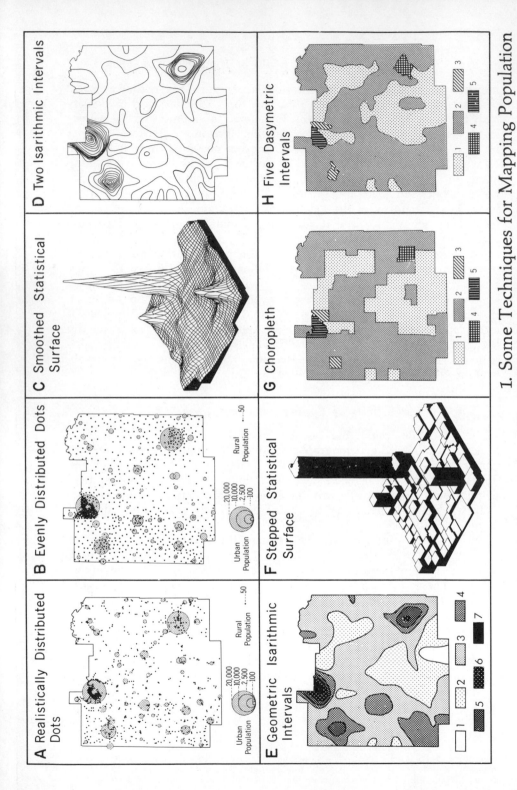

A Realistically Distributed Dots

Urban Population
20,000
10,000
2,500
100

Rural Population ---- 50

B Evenly Distributed Dots

Urban Population
20,000
10,000
2,500
100

Rural Population ---- 50

C Smoothed Statistical Surface

D Two Isarithmic Intervals

E Geometric Isarithmic Intervals

1 2 3 4
5 6 7

F Stepped Statistical Surface

G Choropleth

1 2 3
4 5

H Five Dasymetric Intervals

1 2 3
4 5

1. Some Techniques for Mapping Population

The problems and techniques of population mapping closely resemble those of other classes of statistical mapping, except for the special difficulties posed by the extremely uneven spatial distribution of human beings and the sharp quantitative (and qualitative) differences between urban and rural communities. The eight drawings of a group of counties in central Kansas reproduced here (freely adapted from George F. Jenks, "Generalization in Statistical Mapping," *Annals of the Association of American Geographers*, Vol. 53, March, 1963, pp. 15-26) illustrate some of the more useful approaches to these problems.

Map A is perhaps as realistic a drawing as is possible at the scale used here; it is also one requiring considerable time and effort. Rural population is depicted by means of dots (one dot = 50 rural persons) that are plotted after careful study of topographic or other large-scale maps. Direct field observation might also be employed for the best results. Urban centers are shown by means of proportionally scaled transparent circles or discs. In Map B, another relatively "realistic" drawing, the method is much the same, except that rural dots are evenly and randomly distributed within individual townships instead of being tied to the actual location of people. Note also that the extent of the built-up areas of the larger cities is indicated within their circles.

The smoothed statistical surface shown in Map C is an imaginary surface inferred by interpolation among elevated control points (one surface per township in this instance), and graphically represents population density values that vary smoothly from place to place according to the fictitious but useful assumption of this method. Although seldom used in just this form, the concept of the smoothed statistical surface is basic to the isarithmic method illustrated in maps D and E. These isarithmic maps are analogous to the familiar topographic map in that they show the shape and elevation of a surface—here of a statistical rather than a topographic nature—by means of selected contours. In *Map D*, an isarithmic interval of two was used for areas

with densities of less than ten persons per square mile and an interval of ten was used for those areas with higher densities, the latter because of the steep gradients around the larger cities. In Map E, isarithmic intervals have been selected on a geometric progression, the lower limits of the seven categories being 1.6, 2.9, 5.3, 9.6, 17.3, 31.4, and 57.0 persons per square mile; the number of possible schemes of isarithmic intervals is limitless, the choice depending upon the nature of the data and the specific purpose of the map.

Map F depicts the concept of the stepped statistical surface that underlies the choropleth and dasymetric systems of mapping. In this drawing, the elevation of each prism is proportional to the population density of the particular township that it covers. Thus, the cartographer is able to represent each density value exactly to scale, and no generalization by classing is necessary. More commonly, however, the stepped surface is generalized into several intervals of values, and a choropleth map, such as Map G, is thereby produced. The lower limits of the categories for both maps G and H are 1.6, 5.3, 17.3, 31.4, and 57.0. As is the case in isarithmic mapping, the selection of a specific number of categories and the most effective array of limiting values requires careful judgment.

The dasymetric method illustrated in Map H may be said to represent a more realistic statistical surface (of the stepped variety) than is shown in either the isarithmic or choropleth method. After a careful study of population distribution through analysis of large-scale maps and aerial photos or through field observation, or both, areas of relatively homogeneous density are plotted, with no regard to political or census divisions. Because the mapmaker does not limit himself to just one density value per township, or other unit area, this method is necessarily laborious. If two or more colors are available for use in reproduction, the dasymetric method can be combined with the dot-and-circle method of Map A in order to produce a population map that is perhaps more effective than any other, but also more time-consuming.

cultural facts can be intensely interesting to the population geographer and will be exploited in many ways as he interprets demographic materials.

The list of phenomena presided over by the population geographer can be divided into three categories: (1) the essentially biological; (2) the economic, social, or cultural in causation; and (3) those that constitute the elements of dynamic change. Biological traits are determined by facts of birth, heredity, or the physiological behavior of individuals and are largely beyond the control of the group or individual. They include sex, age, and—assuming adequate objective criteria for its recognition—race. Cause of death, morbidity (the prevalence and type of disease), and various types of physical disability could also be added, despite the significant role of social and cultural factors in their determination. Other aspects of physical anthropolgy, aside from race, might be included, but the facts are seldom available through normal census or registration channels. In any event, data on the biological items of sex, age, and race (or color) are the most widely available, in addition to absolute numbers, even in those statistically backward territories where other types of material are sketchy or altogether missing.

The socially determined population facts are more numerous. These include: residence, occupation (including industry, class of worker, and employment status), place of work, marital status and history, family characteristics (including size, composition, and household relationships), housing characteristics, socioeconomic class and caste, income, literacy, educational status and attainment, reproductive history, place of birth, migrational history, religion, language, ethnic group, nationality, citizenship, military status, and membership in institutional populations. Each of these items is often subdivided into detailed categories, so that the resulting number of possible cross-tabulations of characteristics is extensive; but all or most of these data are available only in those countries with relatively elaborate, long-established census organizations.

The dynamic elements of population include vital events that change the location or gross numbers of people: births, deaths, and movements into and out of a given area. Usually considered as statistical patterns rather than as a succession of isolated events, these phenomena are known as fertility, mortality, in-migration, and out-migration. Population change and its components are as important an aspect of population geography as any other; but unfortunately, this kind of information is often defective or missing. For much of the world, no formal means exists for registering births and deaths; and where there are such registration systems, serious defects are noted in their operation. The quantity and quality of reports on migrational movement are even more limited.

---

acceptable. But virtually no two writers have used the terms "cultural geography," "social geography," and "anthropogeography" in the same way. Some scholars have applied these terms so broadly that they have become synonymous with "human geography," while others have used much narrower interpretations, e.g., cultural geography as the geographic counterpart of cultural anthropology.

Frequently, the population geographer who would analyze the elements of change must strain his ingenuity as he uses indirect means to measure fertility, mortality, and migration.

The problems posed by the cartographic representation of population characteristics are unending; at the same time, few are not encountered in the mapping of other geographic elements, whether cultural, economic, or physical. These problems are particularly acute when it comes to plotting change, either of numbers or of characteristics, and much research remains to be done before the matter is settled. If movement through time is troublesome, then movement through space is doubly so for the mapmaker. The researcher of migration geography will continue to be handicapped until effective visual means are found for expressing the basic data.

CHAPTER TWO

The population geographer
looks at Homo sapiens

Some Pertinent Physical Traits
of Homo Sapiens

The scope and methods of any systematic branch of geography are closely linked to the essential nature of its special subject matter; and so, too, with population geography. What peculiar attributes of Homo sapiens help shape and color this field distinctively?

Insofar as the mass or areal extent of the phenomenon is concerned, no substantive branch of geography deals with anything as physically inconsequential as does population geography. In geomorphology, climatology, soil geography, or the geographic study of cities, agriculture, manufacturing, and many other phenomena, one examines bulky or extensive objects; but human bodies take up an almost infinitesimal fraction of terrestrial space. If the entire human race assembled in a single place and each of the approximately 3.2 billion individuals living in 1964 were allotted a tolerable 0.25 square meter of land surface on which to stand, then only about 800 square kilometers (308 square miles), or 0.00061 per cent of the ice-free land surface of the planet, would be needed. The entire human population of the earth could stand in New York City, and 18 square kilometers (7 square miles) of vacant surface would still remain unused. If one were eager to conserve even more space, it would be possible for 3.2 billion men, women, and children to fit without any crowding into a cubical box with sides approximately 800 meters, or 2,500 feet, long. Even more startling is the realization that the sperm and ova from which all living persons were fashioned could be packaged in a container of a few cubic centimeters that would fit readily into an infant's hand. Obviously, human populations would deserve little attention if they were judged by physical mass alone or by the criterion of visibility, but the visible and invisible effects of our species upon the earth's surface are incalculably greater than the simple physical mass of humanity suggests. A lively appreciation of the infinite ramifications of the development of man's cultural capacities lies at the root of population geography.

However great and overbearing is the cultural superstructure erected with his rather limited physical capabilities, it must be remembered that as a member of the animal kingdom, man has certain distinctive zoological traits that the population geographer cannot ignore. The most pressing concern perhaps is the biology of human reproduction. Man's reproductive capacity and behavior, not considering cultural modifications, are atypical, though far from unique. Human beings become sexually active later, bear smaller litters at longer intervals, are fertile for a longer period, and survive longer after the reproductive years than most other mammals; but in each instance there are other species that equal or exceed the human range. Even though the rate of human reproduction is relatively slow by general mammalian standards, it still produces considerable growth within a single lifetime and enormous ecological pressures in short periods. The human female is usually capable of childbearing for a 30-year period, from about age 15 to age 45 (the male is potent for an even longer period); and if no restraints were placed on sexual opportunity, a woman might produce 20 or more offspring before menopause. In actuality, numerous cultural factors limit the number of children. Even so, an average completed fertility of 10 or more children has been recorded for many groups. The human infant is the most helpless of creatures at birth and remains dependent on adult assistance for an extraordinarily long period. Even among primitive societies the child is not ready to fend for himself until puberty, and in the most advanced societies the period of dependency may last until the late teens or even the twenties. Nevertheless, the survival rate for human children is unusually high by mammalian standards.

Population history is replete with examples of exploding human groups. There is good evidence that since the time of effective European contact, the population of both the Philippines and Indonesia has increased at least tenfold. The population of Russia has multiplied sixfold in the past two centuries and the inhabitants of Great Britain five times just in the nineteenth century, both in the face of substantial emigration and war casualties. Even more striking examples of the human reproductive potential are found in the New World: A population of approximately one million persons in the southeastern segment of the United States two centuries ago has generated a group currently numbering about 50 million, despite minimal immigration and substantial movement to other portions of the nation. The French Canadian population has multiplied on the order of 100 times in the course of 200 years without the benefit of any appreciable immigration.

Homo sapiens has some unusual attributes that have enabled him to achieve a unique degree of ecological success—virtual mastery, indeed, of the greater part of the earth's land surface. The first trait, shared with other primates, is a striking lack of physical specialization for any particular habitat or type of activity. A creature of medium size, man lacks any sort of natural armor, either thick hide or heavy pelt, and has fangs and claws of dubious merit in battle; he is not particularly fleet of foot, is an indifferent swimmer, a hopeless burrower, and is clumsy in arboreal locomotion—altogether a rather sorry zoological specimen and fair game for specialized predators large or small. If this were the sum of his physical qualifications, man would probably still be closely confined to his initial home, if, indeed, he had managed to survive at all.

Fortunately, biological evolution has blessed man with a truly upright posture, giving him free range over the surface of the planet and allowing forepaws to develop into highly adaptable hands capable of a multitude of tasks. Quite late in evolutionary history, a vegetarian prehominid became an omnivorous human being, possibly through a series of abrupt mutations. Although there are some plant foods that his alimentary equipment cannot handle, no other animal can, and does, chew, swallow, and digest as enormous a variety of foodstuffs as man. In recent millennia, the human diet has been enlarged by cooking and chemically treating otherwise poisonous or inedible raw plant materials.

All in all, man's essential lack of environmental specialization together with an inherently great plasticity for coping with a wide assortment of physical milieus has been inestimably valuable to him. Some extreme examples of man's adaptability are the groups of relatively primitive people who manage to survive in the far north of Greenland as well as in the steamy swamps of New Guinea. Others have lived in such opposite altitudes as the Dead Sea trench several hundred feet below sea level, intermittently occupied since prehistoric days, and aboriginal huts in the Peruvian Andes five kilometers above sea level.

Like all other living things, man is the host for a distinctive set of parasites and diseases. The pattern of human pathology has been strongly modified by cultural practices, but disease has been a minor deterrent to the conquest of the globe, interesting and important enough to give rise to the study of medical geography, but a subsidiary issue for the population geographer.[1]

Man as a Cultural Being

The major attribute responsible for the spectacular human achievement is, of course, an unparalleled cerebral development. The quite sudden appearance of the human brain is still difficult to explain beyond

[1] There is a great deal of literature on specific aspects of medical geography and on human physiological reactions to various elements in the physical environment. Two of the more comprehensive treatments are Jacques M. May, *The Ecology of Human Disease* (New York: MD Publications, 1958) and Maximilien Sorre, "L'Organisme humain en lutte contre le milieu vivant," in *Les Fondements de la géographie humaine, I, Les Fondements Biologiques* (Paris: Colin, 1947), 291-409.

the near certainty that a new posture, a ground habit, and the challenge of manual dexterity had much to do with it. This greatly enlarged mental capacity has turned man into a creature qualitatively as well as quantitatively distinct from all other animals, for he is capable of much learning and remembering and thus of devising complex behavioral patterns. Cultural behavior of a sort, i.e., learned behavior passed on by observation to other members of the group, is not entirely unknown among some of the more clever mammals, but it remains at a rudimentary level and shows little areal variation. Culture, as the source of man's versatility and terrestrial supremacy, has been dealt with so often and so effectively by anthropologists and cultural geographers that there is no need to belabor the matter,[2] only to note that human achievement would have been much less sensational had not a cultural capability been accompanied by the unusual plasticity of the human organism. Clearly the population geographer must remain attentive to developments in the field of animal ecology, but the ecology of human beings is such a special subject that there is only minimal overlap of the two disciplines.

Two other nonbiological characteristics of mankind have created special methodological problems for the population geographer: the exceptional variability of population through time and space, and the intensity and diversity of the relations between demographic and nondemographic phenomena. In no other geographic field do the raw data change so radically and so rapidly. This, in turn, means that static information is totally inadequate for grasping either past or present population patterns or the processes that have molded them.

Not only do human populations have a high volatility, but they react to their social and physical environments with a vigor and complexity that is probably unique among geographic elements. For example, the phytogeographer in trying to explain a given plant cover is chiefly concerned with the external factors acting upon plant organisms, much less with the interaction among individual specimens or species, and only slightly with the impact of plants upon environing factors that, in turn, will modify plant life. But human populations are as much active modifiers, consciously or not, of their surroundings as they are passive receivers of outside influences. In this complicated give-and-take, the phenomenon of "feedback" plays a major part. What is done by a human group to a given environmental factor may react upon the group to dampen or amplify their further conduct toward that factor, until some kind of equilibrium is attained or until a qualitative change is made in

---

[2] Among the many explorations of the concept of "culture" and the role of culture in human affairs made by anthropologists, some of the more outstanding are Leslie A. White, *The Science of Culture* (New York: Farrar, Straus, 1949), Alfred L. Kroeber, *The Nature of Culture* (Chicago: Univ. of Chicago, 1952), and Clyde Kluckhohn, *Mirror for Man* (New York: McGraw-Hill, 1949). For a stimulating essay on the relevance of the cultural factor to geographic studies, see Philip L. Wagner and Marvin W. Mieksell, "General Introduction: The Themes of Cultural Geography," in *Readings in Cultural Geography* (Chicago: Univ. of Chicago, 1962), pp. 1-24.

either the human group or the nondemographic factor that will lead on to other processes. The train of events occasioned when a starving, desperately pressed agrarian group subjects an overburdened soil to destructive treatment is a case in point.

A further complication is a close-grained interdependency of population characteristics within a group. Not only are the individual population traits in a complex state of dynamic tension with a variety of (nondemographic) human and physical factors, but they are also so closely interwoven with almost all other population traits that few, if any, can be altered without major reverberations for all the others. The population geographer must, then, resign himself rather early to the fascinating but trying fact that population phenomena are as much cause as effect.

CHAPTER THREE

Problems in finding
and handling data

The Pitfalls of Official Demographic Data

The nature of population geography is conditioned by the form and substance of the data at its disposal as well as by the inherent character of its subject matter. The field is distinguished by an exceptionally strong reliance upon official sources for its basic information. There is nothing unusual about using government documents in geographic work, but the utter reliance of population studies on such documents is rare. It is the nature of the phenomena, not the student's lack of enterprise, that explains this fact.

Except in microstudies, where an individual or a small team of investigators might, with luck, collect material adequate at least for the current situation, the physical requirements of direct observation may be too difficult for the independent investigator. But the techniques of random field sampling, successfully exploited by economic and settlement geographers, do offer interesting possibilities. In the study of some population characteristics, interviewing or observing a carefully chosen sample could be handled by a very small group of fieldworkers so as to yield the desired facts about the total universe. On the other hand, some characteristics of a population may vary so complexly or abruptly through space that nothing less than a complete canvass will do.

Most complicating of all is the fact, already noted, that population phenomena are too dynamic to be studied advantageously at any given instant in time, so that one must usually consult the full historic range of records. Thus, unless he is willing to carry on field work for prolonged periods over a restricted tract or perform equally difficult feats, the lone scholar must turn to the resources of government organizations.

Even there, the intrinsic problems of collecting sound data for large areas are considerable. Many relatively poor nations lack the funds necessary for elaborate census and registration systems; and where capital and intentions are adequate, statistical personnel and tradition are not easily come by.

Are population studies impossible in the absence of official data? Not entirely. If nondemographic, particularly economic, data are published for a nation, one can deduce from them certain probabilities about population traits—if certain assumptions are valid. In the interval between the 1939 and 1959 Soviet enumerations and up to the moment when the results of the 1953 Chinese census were released, the Russian and Chinese populations were estimated by ingeniously juggling many facts on economic production and consumption, voter registration statistics, and the like. For relatively primitive populations, past or present, something can be inferred of population size and distribution from what is known of the exploitative technology of the culture in question and the carrying capacity of the land in terms of that technology. In those fortunate cases where population figures are missing but large-scale maps or aerial photography are on hand population can be counted and pinpointed.[1]

When the student wishes to trace the historical geography of population in an area before the earliest reliable statistics were available, a variety of indirect devices can be adopted. Because Egypt's geology, archaeology, and early human ecology have been vigorously studied, we are able to reconstruct the prehistoric population patterns of the land, at least in outline, by considering what is known of early climate, plant and animal life, and human cultures. For the dynastic period, various archaeological and written records would supplement what is known of the early Egyptian agricultural economy to yield some approximation of patterns and trends. The amount and detail of written records would increase in recent centuries until the first fragmentary statistics of the nineteenth century would come into view followed by the relatively detailed maps, photos, and population data of the current century. At worst, such an exercise would justify itself by throwing our present brief period of statistical literacy into some usable frame of historical perspective.

The student is constantly vexed by limitations and inadequacies in the official data with which he works. Even in advanced nations where great quantities of facts are made available through various agencies there are still problems for the scientific worker because the figures were collected for the specific purpose of the agency concerned, seldom for a scientific reason. Much more burdensome is the fact that reliable population information has come into being so late for such a great part of the inhabited world and that it is still missing or grossly inade-

---

[1] Take, for example, the enumeration and plotting of Liberia's population by Philip Porter through a count of huts on air photographs.

quate for so many areas.[2] Even now there are no usable enumerations or meaningful official estimates of the populations of Ethiopia, Liberia, Somalia, Lebanon, Syria, Afghanistan, Bhutan, Laos, Cambodia, western New Guinea, the two Vietnams, or most of the principalities of the Arabian Peninsula. Only by exercising extreme charity can one accept at anything near face value much of the material published for tropical (especially Spanish and former French) Africa or certain portions of Latin America; and unconscionably long periods have passed since the last complete counts in such places as Uruguay or Burma.

Census-taking and the perpetual inventories of populations represented by adequate registration systems are sophisticated devices that can be handled only in or by advanced societies. Rudimentary approaches to such systems were essayed by the Roman Empire and by the imperial governments of China and Korea long ago, and census or registration systems of sorts were operated by ecclesiastical and municipal authorities in medieval Europe; but a genuine national census did not appear until the eighteenth century in Scandinavia, Prussia, and the United States. Demographic ignorance was gradually overcome by the technical and cultural influences of Northwest Europe throughout the nineteenth century; but not until the current postwar period—with the 1950 Pan American census program, the filling in of several African gaps, and the addition of China, Nepal, Iran, and Iraq, among others, to the roster of census-taking nations—was there a semblance of worldwide coverage. However, in many instances registration systems are still so new and experimental that the results are of limited use. In the United States, for example, vital statistics for the entire national territory have become available only since 1933; there is still much underreporting, though fortunately, in this case the margin of error can be estimated with some confidence.

Even where there are official published data on population, the material is frequently defective. There is an element of doubt for many areas in the simplest of all population items—the absolute number of inhabitants—and as increasingly complex information is considered with the need for greater skill on the part of the enumerator and more knowledge on the part of the respondent, credibility often decreases. As a general rule—with conspicuous exceptions—there is a positive correlation between the level of socioeconomic development of an area (and hence its statistical technology) and the reliability (and abundance) of its demographic information. Among peoples of relatively limited technological attainment, there are difficult problems beyond the administrative ones of finding necessary funds and personnel: ignorance, suspicion, hostility, and occasionally, downright deceit on the part of those being counted; quite often a poorly developed sense of time or magnitude;

[2] The availability of information, past and present, is discussed in Forrest E. Linder, "World Demographic Data," in Philip M. Hauser and Otis Dudley Duncan, eds., *The Study of Population: An Inventory and Appraisal* (Chicago: Univ. of Chicago, 1959), pp. 321-60.

the physical difficulty of gaining access to remote areas; and the usual lack of corollary data against which validity of the population figures can be checked.

Significant changes in national boundaries make it difficult to approach the historical aspects of population. Poland, Germany, and Yugoslavia are only three among the more outstanding examples. Even more universal are boundary revisions among internal political and census districts. Revisions of definitions or categories of population characteristics are also major hazards, particularly when they are arbitrary, though they often mean refinements in statistical technique or recognition of shifting demographic conditions. The intrusion of political factors is shown in the gross shortcomings of the 1870 enumeration of the American South, with its disturbed social and political conditions, or in the deliberate padding of the results of Guatemala's 1940 census for the glorification of the national administration.

Problems of International Comparability

When the geographer deals with two or more nations, major incompatibilities in defining characteristics or in further categorizing specific traits are the rule rather than the exception. This is most obvious in working with economic, social, or cultural facts. Deep intercultural differences in economic (and hence, occupational) structure, marital and family patterns, class hierarchies, or educational systems would, in any case, make simple international comparisons difficult. In another direction, the problem of converting one currency into another and allowing for nonmonetary sources of income make it hazardous to study on an international scale areal variations in income or levels of living.

There are, moreover, many needless obstacles in the path of the population geographer occasioned by failure to standardize what could be standardized, e.g., literacy, migration (international as well as internal), religion, language, or ethnic group. The problem of arriving at internationally valid criteria for urban and rural residences is especially knotty. The diversity of settlement forms and practices among nations is real enough; but it is unquestionable that many official definitions are quite arbitrary and could be made to conform more closely with those of neighboring lands with no injustice to the true nature of the residential structure.[3] There are enough cleavages among national methods

[3] The definition of urban places may be based on (1) size of place, (2) political or administrative status, (3) various social, economic, or other functional criteria (such as existence of central water supply, schools, post offices, or other facilities, or (4) some combination of the foregoing. There is surprising diversity of practice in applying even so apparently simple a concept as size of place. In Japan and the Ryukyu Islands, urban municipalities (*shi*) usually have 30,000 or more inhabitants and may include large rural areas as well as the urban cluster; and in Greece, a municipality or commune having 10,000 or more inhabitants in its largest population center is classed as urban. At the other extreme, towns and industrial centers with more than 400 inhabitants are called urban in Albania; and the Swedes regard as urban built-up areas with at least 200 persons and usually not more than 200 meters

for collecting and reporting data on births and deaths that this material must be reviewed quite critically. Fortunately, a series of international agreements on classifying and reporting causes of death has minimized confusion over this inherently complex phenomenon, although the reliability of diagnoses in some parts of the world is still doubtful.

The question of international comparability extends to the biological as well as to the social aspects of population. There is a notorious lack of international consensus as to how to handle the physical races of mankind in census enumeration. One might expect age reports to be proof against official whim, but here, too, it appears that few nations publish data for single years of age and that the age brackets used, particularly in less advanced countries, sometimes foil attempts at international comparisons. The number and the sex of individuals seem to be the only two characteristics immune to the vagaries of national statistical systems. This discussion should not close, however, without noting that significant steps toward standardizing the census procedures of much of the world have been taken through the efforts of various international scholarly groups, the United Nations, and the Pan American Union.[4]

Political vs. Functional Areal Divisions

The areal subdivisions of nations for which population data are published are seldom ideal from the geographer's point of view, even if one ignores for now the many international boundaries, such as those of tropical Africa, that demographically make no sense. Ordinarily, there is a spatial hierarchy of at least three or four levels of magnitude for these data, from the primary civil division (state, province, department, and the like) down to the small locality, individual settlement, or even, in the case of many larger cities, the urban neighborhood. With few exceptions, the boundaries of such reporting areas are identical to those of administrative districts. If these boundaries have been in existence for a long while, they may once have had some relevance to geographic reality; but often in the course of time they have come to bear little relation to the altered location or activities of the population. The traditional counties of the British Isles are a good example, although instances can be found in most nations. Or if administrative boundaries are newly drawn, the demographic anatomy of the territories was prob-

between houses. How to delimit the outer boundaries of such places and whether to use corporate lines or some variety of functional boundary are also questions to cause international differences of opinion.

[4] In particular, major strides have been made toward standardizing the various enumerations and tabulations carried on during or near the year 1960 in the world as a whole (the 1960 World Population Census Programme) and in Latin America in particular. The specific recommendations are to be found in *Principles and Recommendations for National Population Censuses,* Statistical Papers, Series M, No. 27, UN Publication Catalog No. 158.XVII.5 (United Nations, 1958) and *Programme of the 1960 Census of America. Report on the VI Session of COINS,* Inter-American Statistical Institute (Buenos Aires, 1958).

ably disregarded or unknown. The states and counties of the United States, Canada, Australia, and other recently colonized countries are the most obvious, though not the sole, offenders.

On the other hand, statistical and functional units may coincide nicely at the local, or village, level in rural tracts that have stagnated for centuries. Such is the case for many of the *municipios* of Latin America or the parishes or their equivalents in the more out-of-the-way corners of Western Europe. The new system of Census County Divisions recently set up in several states by the U. S. Bureau of the Census attempts to seek out American approximations of such cells of rural stability. The most startling incongruities between fact and administrative fiat are found in the border zones of growing cities. Here urban residence and function have generally spilled far beyond the political bounds of the metropolis; and if urban growth is rapid, no amount of technical alacrity can keep census divisions abreast of the actual urban-rural frontier. But several of the more statistically progressive nations have labored over this problem: Witness the system of Standard Metropolitan Statistical Areas and of Urbanized Areas in the United States or the "conurbations" of England and Wales.[5]

The limitations of anachronistic or arbitrary boundaries for census districts can be reduced by judicious exploitation of large-scale maps and aerial photography where they are available, or by field observations of the areas in question; but areal discordance between population facts as they exist in real space and as they are reported for heterogeneous districts in census bulletins remains a serious problem for the student.

The areal packages in which population materials are delivered to the geographer are seldom those he would specify were he granted a free choice. If he is interested in less than the entire inhabited earth—which is normally the case—how is he to limit the study area? Must he stop short at official national or subnational boundaries, or should he

[5] The Standard Metropolitan Statistical Areas (SMSA's) employed by the U. S. Bureau of the Census for the 1950 and 1960 enumerations are essentially defined as "a county or group of contiguous counties which contains at least one city of 50,000 inhabitants or more or 'twin cities' with a combined population of at least 50,000. In addition to the county, or counties, containing such a city or cities, contiguous counties are included in an SMSA if, according to certain criteria, they are essentially metropolitan in character and are socially and economically integrated with the central city." The "urbanized area" concept employed in the same census enumeration corresponds to the "conurbations" recognized in certain other countries. In this case the outer limits of the contiguously "urban fringe" surrounding cities of 50,000 or more meeting certain specifications of population density have been delimited either by field surveys or by studying the results reported for small census enumeration districts. For further details and general discussion, see U. S. Bureau of the Census, *U. S. Census of Population: 1960. Number of Inhabitants, United States Summary, Final Reports PC(1)-1A* (Washington, 1961), pp. xix-xx, xxiv-xxvii. The British conurbations are described in General Register Office, *Census, 1951, England and Wales, "Report on Greater London and Five Other Conurbations"* (London: H.M.S.O., 1956). The problem of the areal delimitation of the metropolitan areas is handled in illuminating fashion in International Urban Research, *The World's Metropolitan Areas* (Berkeley and Los Angeles: Univ. of California, 1959).

somehow contrive borders more nearly matching the shapes of genuine demographic-geographic regions? For a study covering only a fraction of a single nation, the choice theoretically hinges upon the nature and purpose of the study, even though in practice it is easier, if not better, to fit the investigation into official reporting areas. For a study involving the entirety of one or more nations, the geographer need have fewer qualms over settling for international boundaries. Even though nation-states do not necessarily crystallize into distinct, tightly integrated regions, there is a certain coherence in the economy and society of a nation, particularly the stable, long-established nation, that carries over into its population traits. Economic and social interaction among the several parts of a nation imposes at least rudimentary national similarities among these sections. Internal political or census boundaries have, on the other hand, only negligible effects on population behavior.

An international boundary often bisects a region with a distinct identity but manages to create, sometimes within a surprisingly brief period, a sharp demographic discontinuity. The border zone (let us call it A-1) of Nation A may have much more in common with the adjacent border zone (B-1) of Nation B, than it does with A-2, a distant province of Nation A. But as one crosses the border line, one also crosses a genuine demographic frontier, not just a statistical artifact. We usually find that A-1 shares more characteristics with A-2 than it does with B-2 at the other end of Nation B, and that despite some strong resemblances, A-1 cannot be mistaken for B-1. There is good reason, then, to accept Nation A as a valid study unit, even though one might take sidelong glances at Nation B and others from time to time. Many illustrative instances could be cited here, among them the United States-Mexican border, the border of the Soviet Union and its Moslem neighbors to the south, or the borders separating the two halves of Germany and Korea.

When all the difficulties in obtaining and using population data are itemized systematically, the reader may feel discouraged. It is important to point out that the data problems of the population geographer are no greater than those of other systematic branches of geography, though they do differ considerably in kind and are perhaps more immediately apparent.

Ultimate Aims:
The Particular or the General?

The definition of its nature, purposes, and limitations would clearly indicate that population geography shares with other divisions of the field the threefold function of description, explanation, and geographic analysis, but markedly diverges from them in the quite unusual attributes of its subject matter, i.e., demographic man. Human beings are slighter in mass, more susceptible to rapid quantitative, qualitative, and locational change, and more likely to react intensely and complexly with many phases of their physical and cultural milieu than is the case with the items studied by other systematic geographers. But thus far no mention has been made of the ultimate aims of the population geographer and whether these aims deviate significantly from those of his colleagues. Is he intent upon discovering immutable, universal laws describing the geographic behavior of populations, or is he content with interpreting unique individual areas? The answer here must be the same as it is for other phases of geography.

Whatever problem or area the scientist may be observing, he habitually seeks valid general propositions or "laws." If a regularity of pattern is suspected in certain geographic aspects of population, and if this suspicion survives trial as a working hypothesis to blossom into a full-blown theory that seems to fit all known cases, then such a formulation could be extremely valuable, less as an end in itself than as a tool for grasping more fully the geographic character of the inhabited earth and its various regions. It is this understanding—the comprehension of reality —that is the ultimate purpose of the discipline. The sometimes quixotic quest for general laws is only one road to this goal. Furthermore, the usefulness of any general laws in the present instance may be limited by the intensity and variety of interaction with other factors that seems to characterize population phenomena. Such complexity of behavior denotes relatively strong individuality for specific areas and wide, if potentially explainable, departures from predicted patterns. There may, then, be no simple formulas to explain the geography of the world's population; at best, only useful fragments of such laws may be available.

PART 2 *distribution of the world's population*

CHAPTER FOUR

Some preliminary experiments in explanation

Why are people unevenly distributed over the surface of the earth? Why does the population map show so many persons living here and so few there? [1] These obvious questions are the kind the population geographer may expect frequently from many quarters. Although explaining the "where" of people is not his ultimate objective, it is a strategic way of approaching the more substantive problems facing the student. There are several reasons for this:

(1) By describing and explaining the location of people, the student capitalizes on a strong, pre-existent, naive curiosity found among scientists and lay persons alike.

(2) The answers to this question may very well have substantial practical value for businessmen, government officials, administrators, planners, and social scientists.

(3) The absolute number of inhabitants is the one population item for which there is some sort of information—even if only in the form

---

[1] No general population map of the world, i.e., one showing absolute numbers or population densities, is offered here for two specific reasons: (1) A truly useful map would require too large a scale for convenient inclusion in a book of this format. (2) The compilation of an adequate map would require an inordinate amount of labor, and the chore would not be consistent with the purposes of this volume. A useful, though far from ideal, series of maps of the entire world appears in Friedrich Burgdorfer, ed., *World Atlas of Population* (Hamburg: Falk, 1954). Representative of the maps in the better current atlases—though, again, by no means fully satisfactory—are *Goode's World Atlas*, 12th ed. (Chicago: Rand McNally, 1964), pp. 20-21; *The Prentice-Hall World Atlas*, 2nd ed. (Englewood Cliffs: Prentice-Hall, 1963), p. 1; and *The Oxford Home Atlas of the World* (London: Oxford Univ., 1955), pp. 98-99. Recent wall maps of world population contain almost as much detail and are not of much more utility than the atlas maps. The largest wall-map distributor in the United States lists five recent items in the current catalog that merit a place in the classroom if not in a research collection: Denoyer-Geppert Company, *Special Area and Foreign Published Maps*, Catalog FM63g (Chicago, 1963), pp. 55-56.

of estimates—for nearly the entire world. For all other characteristics, some of which are quite as important as population size, data are less abundant and usually far less reliable.

(4) The procedures used to account for the whereabouts of people also generally apply to the study of other aspects of population. If we learn how to explain numbers, more than half the battle has been won in explaining the location of age groups, literacy, mortality, and the like.

(5) If the geographers can hardly explain the number and location of a population without touching on most other demographic characteristics in a suggestive way, a truly conscientious effort would evolve into a full-fledged population geography. Such a wide-ranging study would, in turn, take up the many nondemographic phenomena that are in some manner causally linked to population. In other words, one cannot fully comprehend why people live where they do without learning almost everything that is to be known about the society and area in question. An excellent way for the teacher to introduce students to the geography of a region is to display a good map of population distribution and to speculate with them about the origins of the patterns shown therein.

Some Basic Assumptions

Before looking at some possible ways to explain the areal pattern of population numbers, four assumptions should be made explicit:

(1) Adequate locational information in tabular, verbal, or above all, cartographic form is assumed. A curious, generally unnoticed fact is that the typical population map shows *number of individuals* and ignores completely the actual mass or quality of these persons. A coal production map depicting number of lumps rather than tonnage or caloric equivalents would be a genuine oddity, as would a map of forest resources showing number of individual trees rather than board-feet or some other quantitative measure. In industrial geography, the use of maps showing number of plants is much less common than those illustrating actual or intrinsic productivity. It is easy enough to prove that in terms of sheer physical mass a random group of 1,000 Norwegians would probably weigh more than a group of 1,500 or more Congolese Pygmies whose build would be slighter and whose average age would be much lower; on any objective scale of socioeconomic effectiveness, the disparity would be great. However, the population map is doggedly democratic and gives equal weight to equal numbers of each group.

(2) Another assumption—a rather weak one—is that the locational meaning of "live" or "inhabit" as used in population geography is clearly understood. In practice, population students generally accept the usages of local statistical agencies who may specify the location of individuals by their physical whereabouts, i.e., sleeping quarters, at the moment of enumeration, by usual place of residence as of this date (de facto residence), by their more permanent location (de jure residence), or by some form of legal residence not necessarily identical with customary

residence. A related problem is the delineation of "inhabited" as opposed to "uninhabited" space. The area immediately occupied by human beings or constantly used by them is extremely limited, but there is no widely accepted formula whereby the larger areas essential to human existence and well-being can be set off from those that are unused or at best of marginal utility.[2]

(3) It is taken for granted that the biologically determined capacity for survival will vary widely from one individual to another; but these individual differences are evened out when groups of any magnitude are considered, except for a few minor, poorly understood physiological traits that seem to show some interracial variance. Consequently, the human organism is regarded as a constant throughout this discussion.

(4) That any explanation, with the rarest exceptions, will be historical in nature is probably the most basic of all these assumptions. Obviously, it was only through the operation of processes over time and often under conditions quite different from those prevailing now that present day phenomena came into being. Consequently, we must study all available evidence for past events and patterns that may have affected a period. This is a truism not yet sufficiently appreciated and practiced that applies equally well to other branches of geography. *The axiom that all good population geography is, ipso facto, historical geography should be understood to apply to this entire work.*

The "Demographic Bookkeeping" Approach

An obvious way to explain the number and location of people is the rigidly mechanistic approach. Given that all populations are in a state of constant, usually rapid, flux and that the number of people in any given area is simply the sum over time of births and in-migrations less deaths and out-migrations, then the magnitude of its population can be explained simply by demographic bookkeeping. It is true enough that only very few localities have kept good records of vital events for periods sufficiently long to permit such an approach, but it is not unreasonable to hope that eventually we shall have satisfactory data for a large portion of the inhabited world. In the meantime, why not use this method wherever it is feasible?

The answer is that such arithmetical busy-work would satisfy only the least intellectually curious, for it provides only a superficial kind of explanation and ignores the fundamental processes and relations behind vital events. Such "population bookkeeping" does furnish useful preliminary information for the explanatory process, but it does not in itself yield answers of any real substance. It would not be much more ridiculous to say that musical criticism begins and ends with the oscilloscope

---

[2] An excellent demonstration of a possible method for defining and mapping uninhabited areas, and one of the most useful discussions of the problems involved in such a task, is found in Lester E. Klimm, "The Empty Areas of the Northeastern United States," *Geographical Review*, Vol. 44, No. 3 (October 1954), 325-45.

or that literary scholarship should be confined to the statistical analysis of individual letters and syllables. A more fruitful analogy is provided by the study of the origins of landforms, since population numbers of densities can be viewed as a statistical surface of a certain elevation above the datum plane of zero population. For both sets of phenomena, the surface height is the sum of upward and downward movements. Although it would be useful for the geomorphologist to know the precise amount of diastrophic upthrust or downthrust or of deposition and erosion for a large number of discrete parcels of land over a given period, this information would in itself provide only a beginning toward a valid genetic discussion. For both population and landforms a great variety of formative factors are at work well above or below the surface ultimately producing the immediate movements that, in turn, determine altitudes. These less immediate, truly primary factors, and the ways in which they have operated, are what really concern us.

The Effects of the Physical Environment

An entirely different approach that has enjoyed sporadic popularity regards man as the creature of his physical environment. It has been obvious to even the most faithful followers of this doctrine that the elements of environment—climate, landforms, water, soils, minerals, and the biota—can neither singly nor in concert uniquely and wholly deter-mine population numbers or other demographic characteristics. However, they do maintain that its effects are of primary importance in shaping the size and distribution of a population. It is widely accepted that the size, distribution, and morphology of a given plant or animal population are to a great extent governed by physical environment and, of course, history. The reciprocal action of the species upon its environment or its intraspecies relationships would be relatively minor considerations. Changes in the physical environment, evolutionary change within the species, and the general passage of time would greatly complicate cause-and-effect relationships. If enough is known about the physical aspects of that area and the ecological requirements of the plants or animals in question, it is still theoretically possible to predict rather closely the equilibrium conditions of a plant or animal population for a given area.

Human beings, by virtue of their unique cultural capacity, live largely outside the laws of animal ecology. Nonetheless, it takes little reading or field observation, even in the most advanced societies, to discover some distinct causal relationships between the physical environment and certain aspects of human populations. Note such examples as the well-known identification of rich coal basins with dense urban development in Northwest Europe, the magnetic effect of Florida's and California's climates on American migrants, the annual surge of metropolitan resi-dents to seaside and mountains, the close affinity of Chinese peasants for alluvial tracts, the almost universally negative effect of pre-Cambrian outcrops on settlement. In specific instances, one can even forecast population size within quite narrow limits, given adequate data on the critical elements in the physical environment and the nature of the links between these elements and population behavior. The density of the rural population in almost any section of Java or Korea can be predicted with considerable accuracy if the analyst is fortified with certain readily quantified information on extent, slope, and elevation of alluvial surfaces, soil quality, precipitation regime, and length and warmth of the growing season. Similarly, recent studies on the Great Plains have shown a significant relationship, or at least a coincidence, between annual precipitation and thus wheat yield on the one hand, and population on the other.[3] For primitive populations, such as the Eskimos of the American Arctic or the Bushmen of the Kalahari, dependent upon the wild food resources of their habitats, a simple relationship between the supply of game, fish, or plant foodstuffs and human numbers could be anticipated.

The dogmatic environmentalist would admit that cultural differences are significant but still assert that they are transcended by certain universal relationships between environmental factors and human population characteristics. The rapid changes in these characteristics would signify to him the effects of changes in the environment and, more important, an increasingly effective "adjustment" of population to environmental opportunity. If this position has been discredited in recent decades, the opposite notion that population characteristics are shaped almost exclusively by cultural factors is equally untenable. The population geographer must recognize the existence of a valid middle ground. Undoubtedly the physical environment does directly or indirectly affect —and is, in turn, modified by—numbers and kinds of people. The real problem is how and to what extent this is so.

Human Physiology as a Limiting Factor

The question would be much easier to answer if "animal man" could be sufficiently isolated from "cultural man" to observe the interactions of the physical environment with each. Unfortunately, no such phenomenon as an "a-cultural" group of human beings has ever existed. Throughout his history, Homo sapiens has been inseparably tied to culture, and archaeological evidence suggests that even several of the earlier hominid species may have used tools and weapons and indulged in other cultural practices. But even though the behavior of a purely animalian human group in a specified physical setting is by no means clear, enough is known about human physiology to say approximately

---

[3] Arthur H. Robinson and Reid A. Bryson, "A Method for Describing Quantitatively the Correspondence of Geographical Distributions," *Annals of the Association of American Geographers*, Vol. 47, No. 4 (December 1957), 379-91; Arthur H. Robinson, James B. Lindberg, and Leonard W. Brinkman, "A Correlation and Regression Analysis Applied to Rural Population Densities in the Great Plains," *Annals of the Association of American Geographers*, Vol. 51, No. 2 (June 1961), 211-21.

where such a group could or could not survive, at least for brief periods. Man's most immediate physiological need is adequate atmospheric oxygen. After an initial period of adjustment he can live indefinitely, without any artificial aid, as high as 5,000 meters above sea level. At higher elevations—only a minute fraction of the total surface of the earth—brief sojourns are possible only after special training or with the help of supplementary oxygen.

The next most immediate need is a tolerable temperature. A person without clothing or shelter will die after prolonged exposure to temperatures below −5° C (23° F); he can withstand extremely high temperatures for brief periods, but if readings of about 40° C (104° F) or more persist—the level depending on humidity, wind, and shade—death from heat prostration will result. (The optimum thermal range falls between 10° C (50° F) and 30° C (86° F).) The critical figure of −5° C is common at middle and upper latitudes and at high altitudes. The midday temperatures and intense sun in many tropical and subtropical areas are beyond the endurance of the naked human being. But permissible temperatures do occur for a significant portion of the year for almost every part of the world not covered by an ice sheet. Potable liquids and food at intervals of some hours or days are also necessities; but man does have a remarkable dietary tolerance and can subsist almost anywhere outside of absolute deserts.

Certain terrains such as glaciers, shifting sands, some varieties of swamps, and extremely rough or rocky surfaces would make it impossible for "animal man" to survive; and he could not live in the face of such geological hazards as volcanic eruptions, moving ice, tidal waves, or avalanches. But this eliminates only a relatively small part of the earth's surface. A much more important restriction results from man's being a terrestrial animal: Without artificial aids, he can survive in water for only a matter of hours, and there is no instance of any group culturally adapted to a completely marine existence (though it is possible to keep small groups afloat indefinitely). Finally, some areas are closed to our hypothetical "natural" population by predatory animals, certain insects, and endemic diseases. It is likely, then, that far more than half the land surface of the earth would be available as a habitat for "animal man" at least part of the year.

The Actual Human Ecumene

Leaving our discussion of this mythical human population, we might ask what areal limits to human life are found in surveying the real world and its populations, all exploiting in varying degrees their capacities for cultural adaptation. The amazing fact is that man can live, either permanently or for brief periods, anywhere on the earth's surface. Even in A.D. 1500, when many of our techniques for coping with the environment had yet to be devised and the great economic revolutions still lay ahead, the "ecumene," or habitable world of mankind, was surprisingly extensive; and much of it was occupied at one time or another by distinctly primitive groups. Virtually the entire ice-free area of all the continents was inhabited, at least sporadically, except where the surface was too high or poorly drained, or the locality was excessively dry.

Since that date there have been few significant advances of the settlement frontiers, except to some relatively inaccessible or economically marginal oceanic islands such as Svalbard, Bermuda, the Falklands, the Azores (moving back into the 1400's), Mauritius, and a few others. Indeed, there has even been some recession of the frontier through climatic change, economic evolution, or the shattering of aboriginal culture in portions of such areas as coastal Greenland, Alpine Europe, much of Baja California, or sections of arid Australia. Modern technology has made it possible to plant semipermanent scientific and military stations on icecaps and other extreme environments, to have mountaineers live for some days or hours at extreme altitudes, and to establish major mining camps at such improbable places as northern Chile, the Klondike, central Sahara, or the arid coasts of the Persian Gulf.

One can state further that, in general, the direct impact of the physical environment on physical man is a relatively minor issue in population geography. Among the most primitive remnants of mankind, subsisting in areas with few resources, e.g., tundra regions, arid deserts, and humid tropical forests with especially sterile soils, the availability of wild food or the occurrence of climatic and geological hazards are life-and-death matters; the existence of these people hangs by an environmental thread. Elsewhere, cultural mechanisms have been so effective in shielding man from his environment, modifying it, or patching its deficiencies (even helping him ignore it entirely) that we are incapable of relating population and physical environment to each other without appreciating the strange alchemy of culture. This is not to gainsay the value of physiological climatology, medical geography, or similar fields to the population student, but only to assert a dilution of their meaning if they are not exploited in a cultural context. Indeed, so much more needs to be researched on the impact of external environment on morbidity, mortality, and reproduction, on man's thought and imagination, and on the level of human performance in general that it will be some time before the direct effects of the physical milieu upon population behavior can be fully assessed. Present knowledge does indicate that these effects are subordinate to cultural factors, or, in any case, are strongly muted by them. There is also good reason to believe that the degree of primacy of the cultural factor intensifies as the socioeconomic scale is ascended.

The Impact of Physical Factors on Cultural Man

Are there enough common denominators in the cultural behavior of mankind to describe with some general rules the effects of the physical environment, either *in toto* or in terms of single elements acting upon population traits through the medium of cultural complexes? [4] The answer must be a qualified no. The mixture of elements that make up the totality of the nonhuman physical environment is complex. It is exceptionally difficult to devise any sort of statistical index denoting intrinsic population-carrying capacity or any other value of demographic import for an area. The problem is compounded by ethnocentric bias. For example, the ordinary Polynesian's assessment of the optimum population of, say, Missouri, would be far different from the one made by a Chinese peasant; and these divergent world views would certainly carry over into supposedly objective scientific research. Even so, a reasonable consensus is possible for some areas. Human populations *tend* to shun extreme environments (hence the paucity of settlement in Iceland, Newfoundland, French Guiana, eastern Iran, Somalia, Patagonia, or the inner Congo Basin) and *tend* to seek superior environments (Java, the Lake Victoria Plain, or the Valley of Mexico, among many others). But it is easy to find discouraging exceptions: Paraguay is probably superior to Ruanda-Urundi in population potential, but the latter is incomparably more crowded; nature has not favored the Netherlands so much over Louisiana—if it has at all—as the disparity in density figures would indicate; and after a comparison of North Vietnam's natural endowment with that of Iraq, the relative size and density of their populations make no sense.

Any search for a clear-cut correlation between individual physical factors and population density or other characteristics is also disillusioning—with one promising exception. Places that are too small, remote, or inaccessible may remain uninhabited or be visited only sporadically by potential residents regardless of the kind and level of their cultures, even though these places may have valuable resources. Hundreds of small islands in tropical and subtropical waters remain unpeopled despite pleasant, productive climates, ample marine and bird life, and adequate terrain and soils. Inaccessibility, among other factors, has also hindered large-scale colonization of such intrinsically worthy regions as the eastern slopes of the tropical Andes and the Central American highlands, portions of the Peace and Hay river valleys in Canada, the higher Angolan plateaus, and portions of Siberia and the Soviet Far East.

In terms of other physical factors, human numbers generally *tend* to increase with decreasing elevation, increasing rainfall (up to a point), increasing warmth, increasing soil fertility, levelness of terrain, or magni-

[4] The same question is asked in broader terms, i.e., whether there are any pan-human equations describing the impact of the environment on the whole range of human geography, in a provocative new text—George F. Carter, *Man and the Land: A Cultural Geography* (New York: Holt, 1964). Carter holds the physical factor more or less constant by discussing and comparing a number of cultural landscapes occurring within the same general environment. His answer is generally quite negative. It is only fair to add that other human geographers have tackled the same monumental problem, though less directly, and have come up with more equivocal results. Among these authors are Maximilien Sorre, *Les Fondements de la géographie humaine* (Paris: Colin, 1947-52), and Rhoads Murphey, *An Introduction to Human Geography* (Chicago: Rand McNally, 1961).

tude of known mineral wealth. Exceptions to a general rule are so numerous and conspicuous that any dictum on the direct effects of a given environmental element on the pan-human scale is feeble at best. In much of Central America and Andean South America population density rises with altitude; the littoral between Lagos and Accra is one of the driest portions of West Africa as well as one of the most crowded; Flanders and Denmark have dense, flourishing populations despite inherently poor to mediocre soils, while extensive tracts of rich soil in Guatemala, eastern Bolivia, and Iraq beg for colonists. The rough hill lands of Syria are saturated with people, whereas the level plains to the east are empty; the mineral wealth of the Urals is proverbial, but the region is only now becoming a significant node of settlement.

Furthermore, in carefully reviewing apparent correlations, two conclusions almost always are reached: (1) what exists is not a single set of cause-and-effect relationships but rather a number of partially coincident sets; and (2) the relationships are not direct but are filtered through the medium of local cultures and economies. For example, what of the apparent association of coastal regions and high densities? A number of favorable conditions have encouraged economic and population development in coastal areas *under given historical circumstances.* Plains are especially likely to occur in coastal zones, and the coastal plain is conducive to the growth of transport routes and thus of cities. As a border between the terrestrial and marine environments, the coastal region tends to attract those persons, including the merchant, sailor, and fisherman, who can exploit both. Fertile alluvial soils—and dense agrarian populations—tend to occur in littoral zones; such areas tend to have economically useful climates, and for some lands whose over-all climates are poor, it is often the only tolerable area. Where the land has been peopled by overseas migrants, the newcomers often remain in the readily accessible coastal country. For more specific confirmation of this reasoning, examine Australia, Japan, Iceland, Libya, or other nations in which nearly the whole population lives along or quite near the coast.[5]

[5] The tendency for many populations to concentrate along or near coast lines is considered in Josef Staszewski, "Die Verteilung der Bevölkerung der Erde nach dem Abstand vom Meer," *Petermanns Mitteilungen,* Vol. 103 (1959), 207-15.

CHAPTER FIVE

The impact of economic factors

The Economic Factor

Clearly, the economic characteristics of an area exert a much more direct effect upon its population patterns than do its physical characteristics. This happens in two ways: first, the nature of a given economy will, to a great extent, mold the ways in which a group of people will control (or be influenced by) the environing physical elements, either singly or in combination; this process might be termed the resource-nexus. Because the prevailing economic culture posits specific levels and kinds of response to these elements and their various combinations, a given area with given physical conditions at a given time *tends* to have certain numbers of certain kinds of people arranged areally in certain ways with reference to the physical environment. In short, these patterns are logical in terms of both that particular economy and that particular physical complex. This kind of areal patterning is especially noticeable among populations engaged in the primary industries of farming, fishing, forestry, mining, or hunting and gathering. Numbers and patterns alter appreciably as the physical geography of the area is changed, either through "natural" processes or by human action, or as the character of the economy changes. In any case, it is the economy (a human construct whether devised consciously or not) that is active, decisive, and rapidly variable, rather than a relatively impassive, slowly evolving, physical environment. The mining communities of the western United States during the nineteenth century or the sugar-obsessed Lesser Antilles of the eighteenth century forcefully demonstrate this. In both instances population patterns were almost wholly economic in nature, and the great variations in numbers mirrored equally great changes in markets, technology, or recklessly assaulted resources.

Secondly, a particular economic system may *tend* to arrange people in a specific integrative pattern that will require or support a certain population density regardless of irregularities in the character of the physical world in which they live. This second process—the nexus of economic interchange—is the decisive one for most individuals engaged in the secondary and tertiary sectors of an economy, i.e., those employed in the manufacture or distribution of goods or in the provision of various services; but it will also affect the agricultural population of the more advanced countries. Within this nexus of economic interchange, under rules that vary from culture to culture, people *tend* to sort themselves out areally to attain the greatest efficiency, i.e., minimum cost and maximum return, in performing their roles as producers and as consumers of goods and services.

The United States illustrates clearly the operations of these two economic forces. Relatively dense settlement occurs in the rich alluvial valley of the lower Mississippi, in New Jersey's Triassic Lowland, Utah's Salt Lake Oasis, Oregon's Willamette Valley, and in Pennsylvania's York and Lancaster counties and the richer limestone valleys of the Folded Appalachians, but little or no rural population appears in such unrewarding regions as the Adirondacks, the Everglades, the New Jersey Pine Barrens, the Mohave Desert, or the western mountains in general.

On the other hand, if one looks at the enormous density of Manhattan, an island with no agricultural or mineral resources and a meager water supply, or at the large tracts of superb farmland lying idle and untenanted on the outskirts of Chicago, it is clear that we are dealing with another kind of logic. The vast, intricate web of urban society that officially accounts for 70 per cent of the total American population has distributed its citizens with little concern over the physical character of the land it occupies. The percentage is actually much higher if the rural scatterings of city people are realistically included. The initial siting of the now powerful urban nodes and their early fortunes may have been strongly influenced by the lay of the land and the economic logic of an early agrarian society, but the modern urban-industrial network has long since generated its own spatial code.

And so to a striking degree the distribution, characteristics, and movements of our population are responsive to spatial differentials in employment and consumption opportunities as determined by the internal structure and workings of a highly elaborate interlocking economic system. The ultimate sources of the raw materials that enter this system or the direct effects of the physical environment on its operations are minor issues. Geographers and economists have worked hard to chart the spatial lattice of economic activity and the resultant population details; they have been most successful in recent years through the use of central-place theory. That one can ascertain some of the basic tendencies in the location, spacing, relative size, and functions of settlements and their populations now appears to be well-established, even though the ultimate implications of the theory have not yet been fully explored.[1]

The "nexus of economic interchange" works best within a national or subnational framework, but it is also applicable to the international scene. The functions, and hence, size and structure, of such places as Hong Kong, Singapore, Zanzibar, the cities of the Rhine-Scheldt estuary, or Great Britain in general are not comprehensible without considering the transoceanic flow of goods and services through these commercial emporia. A similar case is Megalopolis, the region Jean Gottmann terms "North America's economic hinge" [2] because it performs so many functions for the North Atlantic community as a whole.

The nature and operation of the economy seem to offer much brighter prospects for understanding the size and uneven distribution of human populations than does the direct impact of the physical environment; but such "economic determinism" must be developed cautiously. Two pitfalls are the fallacious assumptions that number of inhabitants is positively correlated with level of economic development or activity, and that universal economic principles govern interaction of people, resources, and economy. There is a general tendency for populations to become larger and denser, other things being equal, as the economic scale is ascended from the most primitive groups to the most advanced. But one need not look far for glaring exceptions. Where a rich biota is readily available, as was the case along portions of the California, Washington, and British Columbia coasts during aboriginal times, preagricultural tribes of limited technological attainment were able to achieve high densities. In contrast, settlement is greatly attenuated in such relatively advanced areas as agricultural Australia or the American Great Plains, although the standard of living is incomparably higher among these few residents than among the Pacific Coast Indians. In rural Kenya, the areas of European tenure contrast greatly with many of the African tribal lands.

Economic behavior varies from community to community, and within one place through time as well. Insofar as population characteristics are economically conditioned, these variations must be appreciated in order

[1] The large and rapidly growing literature on central-place theory is listed, with descriptive annotations, in Brian J. L. Berry and Allen Pred, *Central Place Studies: A Bibliography of Theory and Applications*, Regional Science Research Institute, Bibliography Series, No. 1 (Philadelphia, 1961). Central-place theory and other aspects of the spatial ordering of people and economic activities within the nexus of economic interchange are treated in August Lösch, *Die Raumliche Ordnung der Wirtschaft*, trans. W. H. Woglom and W. F. Stopler as *The Economics of Location* (New Haven: Yale Univ., 1954); Walter Isard, *Location and Space-Economy* (New York: Wiley, 1956); William L. Garrison, "The Spatial Structure of the Economy," *Annals of the Association of American Geographers*, Vol. 49, No. 2 (June 1959), 232-39, Vol. 49, No. 4 (December 1959), 471-82, and Vol. 50, No. 3 (September 1960), 357-73; and Brian J. L. Berry, "Approaches to Regional Analysis: A Synthesis," *Annals of the Association of American Geographers*, Vol. 54, No. 1 (March 1964), 2-11.

[2] Jean Gottmann, *Megalopolis: The Urbanized Northeastern Seaboard of the United States* (New York: Twentieth Century Fund, 1961), especially pp. 102-65.

to understand population behavior. The Western European economic ethos has been tremendously successful, not only in its native habitat, but also in its overseas territories—and now, to a notable extent, in Japan, Eastern Europe, and the Soviet Union. Such a record encourages the assumption that here surely is one of the eternal verities. But the supposedly free play of the market place, the maximization of profit, and the material enhancement of the individual—central tenets of our own economic philosophy—are found in different forms, if found at all, in other societies. These principles do not even operate as purely and uniformly within the Western European culture realm as is often assumed.

Since Homo economicus is a mythical creature, the impact of economy upon demography must be viewed from the standpoint of culture. Economic behavior is only one facet of the broader culture of a group; and the ways in which the people earn their living and consume the fruits of their labor is shaped by a culture's basic orientation. Each culture has a distinctive way of evaluating and using its environment, and arranging economic transactions within the community. Some earlier examples illustrate this. The size and distribution of rural population in both Kansas and Korea are coincident with certain physical properties of those areas. Suppose that the two populations (and economic cultures) were transposed. There is no way of predicting precisely what the Koreans would do with Kansas or the Kansans with Korea; but it is undeniable that the resultant population patterns would differ drastically from the current ones.

History is replete with instances of radical transformations in population patterns brought about by cultural change. Aboriginal North America has a distributional pattern that was, in large part, shaped by economic considerations. It was altered unrecognizably, though the economic motif became stronger than ever, with the introduction of European settlers and culture. This was not simply a quantitative change (there was more than a 100-fold increase in numbers, although aboriginal density declined in some localities); it was a fundamental reordering of pattern. Less sudden but equally profound change can be traced over a 2,000-year period on the population map of Great Britain (guesswork is needed for the first millennium) as invasion and indigenous cultural change revolutionized economic conditions.

Economic Factors and Absolute Numbers: The Ackerman Formula

Given that we fully understand the economy and physical resources of an area within the context of its history and culture, to what extent can we explain population numbers and distribution within the area? Central-place theory has made a promising start in accounting for *relative* disposition of people and functions (though the theory is most successful where physical, cultural, and historical diversities are ignored). Can the economic approach tell us anything about the absolute dimensions of a population? That is to say, can the size of a community be accounted for if enough is known about its economic characteristics and its economic history?

One of the few serious attempts to reconnoiter this approach is a formula proposed by Edward Ackerman: [3]

$$P = \frac{RQ(TAS_t) + E_s + T_r \pm F - W}{S}$$

The symbols have the following meanings:

P —number of people
S —standard of living
R —amount of resources
Q —factor for natural quality of resources
T —physical technology factor
A —administrative techniques factor
S_t—resource stability factor
W —frugality element (wastage or intensity of use)
F —institutional advantage and "friction" loss element consequent
    upon institutional characteristics of society
E_s—scale economies element (size of territory, etc.)
T_r—resources added in trade

It would be extremely difficult, though not quite impossible, to quantify some of the factors of this equation, and equally difficult to gather all the basic information for a given area and period. Nevertheless, a serious attempt to apply the Ackerman approach or something resembling it might seem worthwhile. Unfortunately, basic flaws in a formula like this make it unworkable. At least three major elements in the equation—population size, the resource-technology factor, and standard of living—are not independent of one another; they interact vigorously and complexly among themselves. So, for example, the extent to which known, usable resources are exploited is probably as much a reflection of number of people or standard of living as it is a determinant of these facts. Ackerman was keenly aware of this. However, one must assume that population size is no more a dependent variable in this equation than the other factors are independent variables; it is largely controlled by elements other than those appearing in the formula: the effects of past conditions, the total cultural context, and a variety of unique or accidental occurrences.

The Temporal Factor

The temporal factor, inertia, may well be the most significant of any factor in shaping the size and location of a population. Theoretically, the Ackerman formula can apply either to a succession of economic

[3] "Population and natural resources," in Philip M. Hauser and Otis Dudley Duncan, eds., *The Study of Population: An Inventory and Appraisal* (Chicago: Univ. of Chicago, 1959), pp. 621-48.

phases or just to closely spaced dates in the history of a community; and if one were to accept the existence of a frictionless society, then the formula might explain the changing size of the population. Reality is more troublesome. Economic conditions are normally not experienced in their full demographic impact until some years after they have come into being, and the effects may linger long after these conditions have vanished. Such a time lag is of little consequence in relatively stable societies, but when an economy is undergoing rapid transformation, one must look to the past as well as to the present for the economic rationale of a given demographic situation.

The temporal factor may transcend immediate economic calculations. The main reason that a population of a given size dwells in a given area is that the bulk of it was there in the immediate past—sometimes with, but often without, much economic justification. The momentum of a pre-existing situation will generate its own force, creating social and economic bonds that can make existence in the home region bearable (if not optimal), and will assuage the natural inclination to remain in tolerable, familiar surroundings. If the world's population were temporarily whisked off this planet and then redistributed in compliance with strict economic logic, the new population map would be unrecognizable. In actuality, one must examine the past to understand current population patterns. The phenomena created by past conditions have accumulated to form areas of the world as we now see them. Some of these conditions were economic, many were not; in any case, we do know that they were notably different from present conditions. Let us restate: meaningful interpretations of population facts are densely rooted in time and the totality of human experience.

A serious flaw in the economic approach is the assumption that one can completely explain the statistics of a population if the economic basis of a culture is understood. Even within the terms of the Ackerman equation, standard of living, the frugality element, and the institutional structure of a society are only fractionally economic in character and are fully understandable only in terms of total cultural configuration and value systems. It is apparent that economic conditions may often impinge directly on in-migration and out-migration and only indirectly on fertility and mortality; but it is important to realize that many non-economic, often nonmaterial, factors help to determine all four dynamic elements of population.

CHAPTER SIX

Cultural determinants of population numbers and distribution

Cultural Controls Over Fertility Level

Cultural factors are as important as any others in shaping the size and areal patterns of a population. Among them is the long, interesting list of noneconomic practices, specific for a given culture, that influence the number of births. For example, mating and marital practices can be major determinants of fertility: the absolute and relative ages of spouses at marriage, the degree to which celibacy is encouraged or condoned, the prevalence of plural as opposed to single marriages, customs regarding divorce or the remarriage of the widowed and divorced, dowry and bride-price practices, the institutional framework for mating (civil vs. religious marriage, common-law vs. registered unions, casual visiting relations vs. prolonged cohabitation, etc.), the forms and prevalence of contraception, the sexual division of labor within the family, beliefs concerning relative value of male as opposed to female offspring, specified seasons of indulgence in or abstention from sexual intercourse, the socially ideal number and spacing of children, attitudes toward illegitimate childbearing. In addition, certain technical aspects of the demographic structure, particularly age, sex, and residential composition, are variously determined and, in turn, help mold fertility patterns.

The items listed are not only largely divorced from the economic realm, they also seem somewhat arbitrary. Although some of these practices may have flourished because of distinct survival value, more often they have continued to exist only by force of tradition and for lack of any compelling physical reason to abandon them. The sum total of such behavioral traits is a specific, culturally induced fertility level set anywhere within the broad limits of technology, local resources, and standard of living. This pattern may be directly modified by environmental factors such as the effects of certain endemic diseases on fecundity and fertility or, in the case of a community exhausting its resources and technology, acute environmental stress that reduces fertility through malnutrition and premature death; but normally these are minor considerations. The modern period, from which we must extract nearly all our reliable data, has been one of such stunning economic transformation that demographic change induced by economic factors has done much to obscure intercultural differences in fertility levels. Yet these differences have always been, and still remain, important.

Despite intercultural variety, one generalization seems to hold for nearly all groups: the net effect of cultural patterns upon childbearing is a fertility level significantly below the physiological maximum. Consequently, most human groups have failed in the past to multiply to the limits imposed by local resources and natural enemies. This has not been the case with most animal populations. In the subhuman animal world, members of a species seldom press hard enough against the limits of available sustenance to cause chronic malnutrition, largely because numbers are kept to a comfortable size by occasional outbursts of disease, predation, and a still poorly understood territorial instinct. (The operation of this instinct may trigger physiological changes and a behavioral pattern whereby the individual or group is guaranteed a minimum spatial range.) However, within these limitations, animal populations do tend strongly to reach and maintain the largest size possible.

This phenomenon must be touched on hesitantly for lack of statistical confirmation; but it seems very likely that in aboriginal America, medieval Europe, and most of pre-European (and much of contemporary) tropical Africa, among other regions, human numbers were kept well below the carrying capacity of the land by various cultural checks on fertility. Quite recently, the populations of such countries as Egypt, Ceylon, Taiwan, Korea, and Hispaniola have grown tremendously. That there have been no appreciable changes in technology, resources, or living standards—at least as yet—makes credible the existence of an earlier submaximal population equilibrium. It is also tempting to look at the other side of the coin and speculate how traditionally high birth rates, exceeding normal death rates, may have set off some of the Polynesian migrations across the Pacific or many major movements of tribes outward from the environmentally parsimonious Eurasian interior. In extreme cases, high fertility levels may conceivably lead to such overpowering stress on the habitat and society that impoverishment or destruction will result. Conversely, the same condition may bring about a sudden leap in technology and economic organization in order to provide more ample subsistence.

Culturally conditioned low fertility patterns do occur, but under premodern conditions this has been a temporary, often self-destructive, condition. The reduction of birth rates through mass demoralization was quite likely one of the reasons for the disappearance of numerous aboriginal groups in North America and the Caribbean in the years immediately after European conquest, though waning fertility was overshadowed by the more obvious effects of slaughter and disease. The decimation of many groups in the Southwest Pacific might also have been caused by a sudden drop in fertility rates induced by culture shock. Serious depopulation has recently threatened much of former French Equatorial Africa and the Belgian Congo because of the sharp decreases in fertility in the face of chronic labor shortages.

Cultural Factors in Mortality

A community's cultural personality affects not only the rate at which it produces children but also the odds for survival of its living members. Many deaths result directly from environmental hazards, failures of the economy, accidents, warfare, and other calamities beyond the control of the victims. But after sifting the effects of climate, biota, and natural and man-made catastrophes, a large residue of mortality still remains, the extent and nature of which is shaped by cultural practice. Almost universally, communities strive earnestly, using all known and approved methods, to keep mortality as low as possible; but these efforts are often unwittingly sabotaged by many traditional, apparently harmless customs.

Survival rates for young children and newborn infants, who account for a disproportionate fraction of mortality, are particularly vulnerable to the vagary of tradition. The list of relevant factors is long: practices surrounding the care, feeding, and treatment of the pregnant female; methods of confining the mother and delivering the infant; the routine of nursing and weaning the infant; general nutritional practice for mother and child; the treatment of infant diseases; the clothing and housing of the very young; the practice or avoidance of infanticide; the relative value of male and female children. As the child matures, mortality risks decline considerably, and they begin to rise again perceptibly only in middle age; but throughout his lifetime, an individual's chances of dying, as well as the type of death he encounters, may be partly determined by the kind of community to which he belongs—by range and make-up of diet, food tabus, drink, clothing, shelter, sewage disposal, personal and public hygiene, medical knowledge and practice, restraints on murder and suicide, and by how well, in general, the community can withstand the assaults of climate, insects, bacteria, fungi, viruses, and microorganisms of every description—as well as by means of livelihood and military patterns. Once again there is good reason to suspect intercultural differentials in level and structure of mortality, even though their nature is often masked by more obvious differentials in environment, economic practice, and general population structure, as well as by serious deficiencies in data.[1]

[1] But note the anomalously high male, as opposed to female, life expectancy at birth cited for Ceylon in the Appendix. This is almost certainly a matter of cultural practice.

Intercultural differences in fertility and mortality are still not clearly charted; but recent history makes it certain that they do exist, that they change, and that they may be as potent as economic factors in shaping the size and spatial dispositions of populations. Two distinct, but not unrelated, factors seem to make up the population pattern of any given area: economically determined demographic events (births and deaths, but particularly migrations), and culturally determined demographic events (migration, but particularly births and deaths). This quality of demographic causation is thrown into especially sharp relief during periods of rapid change, when "cultural demography" may flout the logic of "economic demography," or vice versa, each one producing deleterious effects upon the other.

The long, pronounced decline of fertility in the United States (one might also cite France in this connection) from the early nineteenth century until 1940, notwithstanding a chronic shortage of labor, took place in defiance of economic common sense and for reasons still obscure and privy to American social psychology. This decline helped to induce the vast migration out of Europe that began in earnest about 1830, and more recently, helped to start massive migrational currents within this nation. Regional departures from national cultural norms have produced striking disconformities between demographic trends and local economic capability, as can be seen in the heavy out-migration of people from areas such as Utah and the Southern Appalachians, where fertility rates are high and resources are limited. Similarly, the recent dramatic decline in the mortality rates of many "underdeveloped" lands having dense populations, deficits of undeveloped resources, and chronic underemployment is culturally rather than economically induced, and it may well generate unwholesome effects upon land and livelihood within such countries. Conversely, even though the recruitment of numerous young male workers from villages throughout tropical Africa for work in mines, plantations, and urban enterprises has made possible the rapid material advance of a few fortunate regions, their absence has had a decidedly unhealthy impact on the demography of the tribes in question. Indeed, the very survival of some groups has been endangered.

Culture and Migration

Cultural background, probably more than fertility and mortality, is largely responsible for the general migratory propensities of a group, even though the precise details of source, volume, velocity, and destination of migrational flow may be shaped by immediate economic factors.[2]

---

[2] Migrational phenomena have not yet received the attention they deserve from geographers. To date, the most ambitious effort dealing with the subject is in Maximilien Sorre, *Les Migrations des peuples: Essai sur la mobilité géographique* (Paris: Flammarion, 1955). Sociologists and economists have dealt much more extensively with migrational matters. Some major ideas and issues are reviewed and a valuable

This basic migratory pattern is part of the over-all design of a society within which economic, social, demographic, and other types of behavior are enfolded. The mounted nomads of the Eurasian and American plains, or the homeless Gypsies and the immemorially earthbound peasants of the alluvial lands of Southeast Asia, have migratory patterns of opposite extremes, but many intermediate forms of migration can also be recognized. The population geographer observes carefully those societies or segments thereof in which repetitive moves such as nomadism, transhumance, commuting, or seasonal vacations are basic facts of life. But what of the more or less permanent transfers of people into, out of, or within the territory of a community? Here, too, cultural and economic motivations are blended. For example, the extraordinary migratory proclivity of the Irish is only partially justified by economic pressures in the homeland.[3]

Conversely, the reluctance of the French to desert their land in large numbers—even during the past century of golden opportunity—becomes intelligible when one understands France's social and economic history and its national character. The migrations of the Polynesian peoples, many of the tribes in Madagascar,[4] and the Scandinavians (from about A.D. 800 to 1100) were likewise only partly due to economic impetus.[5]

The strength of the individual's attachment to his group may be important in deciding how migratory that group will be. The highly individualized migrants of frontier America and Australia were culturally footloose in the extreme, but the land-poor Indians of highland Guatemala are unwilling to migrate a short distance to the nearly vacant fertile lands along the Pacific slope. Severe social inhibitions, probably more than lack of capital, have held them back.

Among nations of advanced economic attainment, a new cultural factor in migration is emerging. More and more moves are being inspired by the "amenities"—those physical, recreational, and social attractions that draw affluent migrants in quest of more nearly ideal living condi-

---

bibliography is given in Donald J. Bogue, "Internal Migration," and Brinley Thomas, "International Migration," in Philip M. Hauser and Otis Dudley Duncan, eds., *The Study of Population: An Inventory and Appraisal* (Chicago: Univ. of Chicago, 1959), pp. 486-543. For further, annotated listings of the important literature in this field, see Hope T. Eldridge, *The Materials of Demography: A Selected and Annotated Bibliography,* International Union for the Scientific Study of Population and the Population Association of America (New York: Columbia Univ., 1959), pp. 167-91.

[3] Irish emigration has been the subject of many books and articles. For a specifically geographic treatment consult T. W. Freeman, "Population and Emigration," in *Pre-Famine Ireland: A Study in Historical Geography* (Manchester: Manchester Univ., 1957), pp. 13-50, and "Population," in *Ireland: A General and Regional Geography* (London: Methuen, 1960), pp. 118-45.

[4] The standard work on Polynesian migrations is in Peter H. Buck, *Vikings of the Sunrise* (New York: Stokes, 1938). Migration within Madagascar is discussed in Hubert Deschamps, *Les Migrations intérieures à Madagascar* (Paris: Berger-Levrault, 1959).

[5] Of the many essays on Viking history and migrations, one of the most readable and informative is in Johannes Brøndsted, *The Vikings* (London: Penguin, 1960). Pelican Book A459.

tions. Quite possibly, the nature of such pleasurable places may vary from country to country and from one culture to another.

Cultural preferences have often operated decisively in the choice or avoidance of destinations. The historical geography of the Spanish in the New World is a good illustration of this. Settlers gravitated readily to regions that were reminiscent of Iberia in climate, terrain, and plant life, and they shunned the colder, wetter, and swampier tracts for which their ecological heritage had no simple answers. And so the Spanish adapted successfully to the low-latitude highlands and steppes of Latin America, but were reluctant to claim Uruguay, Paraguay, or most of Argentina until late in the colonial era; they never effectively penetrated southern Chile, most of Texas, coastal Georgia and the Carolinas, or Florida. Cultural predisposition is actually only a small, though possibly a crucial, part of the Spanish-American story and it must be used cautiously in commenting on any migratory flow. It is a valid consideration in studying the movements of Chinese emigrants from Fukien and Kwangtung or of overseas Hindus or Britishers. Partially analogous landscape is suspected to be a factor in the New World distribution of Scandinavians, though here, too, a number of other historical and economic items must be considered. On the other hand, to approach the locational pattern of Negro slaves in America in the context of African attitudes would be frivolous. The element of choice was, of course, minimal for these migrants, however it might have operated among the buyers and sellers of slaves.

The Role of Social Avoidances

On the darker side of human nature, deeply rooted intergroup anxieties and hostilities may not only lead to violent action—warfare, genocide, and mass deportations—but may also act continuously through time to inihibit the occupation of otherwise attractive areas. Animosity does not automatically spring up when peoples of different race, religion, language, ethnic affiliation, or even social class or political belief reside near each other, but it is frequent enough to have visibly affected the population map. At its worst, chronic military tension is created along common borders or even mutually shunned no man's lands. This phenomenon might well have led to the patchy population map of aboriginal North America, with its wide zones of fertile, but untenanted, land (Kentucky in 1770 is a good example); and animosity has influenced the disposition of tribal populations south of the Sahara and in many of the rougher upland tracts of South and Southeast Asia.

Intergroup antipathies also affect the locations of more advanced populations, as is illustrated in the mass exodus of both Greeks and Armenians from opposite sides of Turkey during the past several decades, the disproportionate numbers of socially disadvantaged Negroes abandoning the American South in the twentieth century, and the flights of Englishmen from Kenya, Hindus from Pakistan, French settlers from Algeria,

Arabs from Israel, and white homeowners from the older cores of American metropolises. The effects of intergroup antagonism are not always so overt as in these examples, but even when such effects are partially submerged or combined with other factors, they deserve very close attention from the population geographer. Conversely, a "herding instinct" assembled European Mormons within Utah during the past century, brought Jews into Israel in the recent past, and on a more limited scale, moved Armenians into Soviet Armenia after World War II. Furthermore, not all human groups reject the company of alien groups—indeed some are strikingly hospitable. The Brazilian success in achieving so varied and harmonious an amalgam of races and national cultures may stem, in large part, from permissive old-world Portuguese attitudes.

The Role of Physical and Social Disasters

So far, the explanations offered for the unequal global distribution of mankind—the direct impact of the physical environment, the operation of economic factors, and the workings of various noneconomic cultural traits—lead over long periods of time to a state of demographic equilibrium. The remaining genetic factors that mold population size and distribution act quite differently; these are discrete, often unique, events that occur only at particular times in particular places—physical and social disasters, and deliberate decisions, both social and political. Even though disasters follow their own laws of cause and effect and are not without a certain logic of their own, they may appear haphazard and unpredictable to the population student. In any case, they temporarily interrupt basic, long-term trends, and although they leave no lasting mark on the population, their immediate impact can be severe.

Many natural disasters may affect the size and composition of a population: earthquakes, landslides, volcanic eruptions, floods, hailstorms, glacial advances, hurricanes, tornadoes, insect plagues, epidemic outbreaks of new bacteria and viruses, migrations of sand dunes, tsunamis, severe drought, fire (which may be of either natural or human origin), shoreline subsidence, and, rarely, meteoritic falls. These sobering events serve to remind us of the narrow environmental limits within which human life is delicately balanced. No portion of the inhabited earth is completely immune to such disasters, but on the other hand, wherever settlers have firmly established themselves, rarely have they been driven away for protracted periods by natural calamities (if one overlooks shoreline changes and the advances of the Pleistocene glaciers).

In the majority of cases, the effects of such disasters have been relatively local and temporary, however severe they might have been at the moment. Standing in present-day San Francisco, Lisbon, or Tokyo, it is difficult to imagine the havoc caused by historic earthquakes whose traces have been so thoroughly erased—unless those shattering tremors that are possible at any instant should occur again. The peasants in Indonesia and the Caribbean knowingly risk their lives by tilling the lower slopes of treacherous volcanic peaks. An endless series of violent floods in the Yellow River Valley has not dissuaded great numbers of Chinese from resettling the stricken areas. More than four centuries of hurricanes have taken their toll of Antillean life and property without appreciably revising the main outlines of population distribution.[6] In any case, when disaster strikes (excluding epidemics), a random sampling of the local population is affected, leaving little, if any, change in population composition.

Social disasters can be more deadly, prolonged, and areally extensive in impact than natural disasters, and more selective in results. The wholesale slaughter of a major war needs no comment. Less obvious is the selectivity of casualties and the migration induced by warfare in terms of sex, age, class, physical condition, and residence. The immediate effects on size and characteristics of populations can be severe, but the delayed political and economic effects can also be important since they, in turn, have demographic repercussions. Nonetheless, the resilience of human populations in restoring prewar numbers and trends is little short of miraculous. Numerical scars heal within a few generations, and the basic genetic processes of economy and culture interacting with society and the physical earth again hold full sway over demography. It seemed impossible to the survivors of the Thirty Years' War that the populations of the German principalities would ever be replenished; yet the stains of that prolonged blood bath have long since faded from the European population map. In cases like the post-Civil War United States or post-Napoleonic Britain, a single generation may smooth over the more obvious demographic damages. Paraguay is unusual in that almost a century after its population was maimed in wars with its larger neighbors, it still suffers from underpopulation; but in another generation or two the losses will be made good.

Among some relatively primitive groups, warfare is part of the normal way of life and even constitutes one of the elements in their demographic equilibrium. Among nation-states, warfare may be only a sporadic, abnormal event, but it must often be taken into account in studying the population of a particular place during a particular period. There are unfortunate exceptions among modern nations, as in Latin America, where political instability has been endemic in virtually every republic since independence was achieved 60 to 170 years ago. Where this instability has been particularly acute, as in some of the Central American republics, civil disturbances are frequent; and this has been reflected in the size, distribution, and make-up of the population.

Forced Population Transfers

The deliberate destruction or forced transfer of populations are, happily, rather unusual events for most areas, but they do affect the

---

[6] Details of location have been affected, however; the proposed inland relocation of Belize is only the most recent attempt to find safer urban sites.

population geography of some places. Genocide occurred in much of the New World with the deliberate stalking and slaughter of aboriginal groups in the United States, Canada, Brazil, Argentina, and Chile; the experience was repeated in Australia, Tasmania, and portions of South Africa, and among more advanced peoples, in Turkish Armenia. Such butchery has not been confined to subordinate racial and ethnic groups; it has also been directed against religious and political minorities. The extermination of most of European Jewry during World War II is only the most notorious example. The history of medieval Europe is crowded with accounts of the attempted eradication of dissident religious sects; and Islam also had its share of holy wars and sectarian strife in the Middle Ages. Prior to the twentieth century, the greatest forced population move was created by the African slave trade; it persisted from the middle of the fifteenth century to the last half of the nineteenth. At least 15 million people were forcibly taken from their villages and dispatched to the New World; smaller numbers were sent to Iberia and Southwest Asia.[7] Countless others were killed during raids or died en route to the slave markets. Even now, several decades after its cessation, the imprint of the slave trade can still be clearly seen in the number and distribution of tropical Africa's inhabitants. This trade has also greatly affected the population geography of the United States and Latin America. On a lesser scale, there has been forced conscription of Indian laborers in various parts of colonial Latin America—often for work at distant points; and some transfers of laborers in various sections of Southeast Asia have been involuntary.

Since 1910, the nation-states of Europe and Asia have firmly attached themselves to the principle of ethnic homogeneity. Such a bewildering succession of international population transfers have occurred that they very nearly constitute an autonomous field of studies, one quite necessary to interpret the demographic careers of the countries involved. The notion of homogenizing the nations by ejecting unassimilated elements is not entirely modern; it was practiced on a grand scale as early as 1492 with the expulsion of Moors and Jews from the Iberian Peninsula. It is only in recent years, however, that the process has become widely popular and the necessary techniques have been perfected. Almost every European nation has sought to rid itself of ethnic impurities during the twentieth century, occasionally by boundary revision, but much more often by simple deportation or by trading the minority to their mother country for the corresponding minority there. These movements have

---

[7] The nature of the movement means that there can never be any reliable statistics on the volume of the African slave trade. The figure quoted here represents the conservative general consensus arrived at in Robert R. Kuczynski, *Population Movements* (New York: Oxford Univ., 1936), pp. 8-17; Alexander B. Carr-Saunders, *World Population: Past Growth and Present Trends* (New York: Oxford Univ., 1936), p. 48; and Gunnar Myrdal, *An American Dilemma: The Negro Problem and American Democracy*, 2nd ed. (New York: Harper, 1944), p. 12. More recently, in a full-scale study of the African slave trade, the author suggests that Africa was deprived of at least 50 million persons before and after embarkation. Basil Davidson, *Black Mother: The Years of the African Slave Trade* (Boston: Little, 1961).

sometimes been complicated by major revisions of national boundaries and even more so by the mass moves of war refugees, combatants, forced laborers, political refugees, and other displaced persons during and immediately after World War II.[8] The resettlement of such war-driven migrants can now be regarded as nearly complete, and the "repatriation" of ethnic minorities has gone as far as it is ever likely to go. In Asia, massive interchanges of population have taken place between India and Pakistan as have the large-scale repatriations of the Japanese and Dutch from their former colonial holdings, and the reassembling of the Korean diaspora.[9] The effects of such transfers on regional population totals and composition have been striking: the vacuity of western Poland or the Sudetenland in 1946 and the crowding of West Germany are only two examples.

One of the recurrent patterns in modern history has been the exodus of dissident groups during and immediately after internal political upheavals. Citing the European disturbances of 1848, the American, French, Russian, Chinese, and Cuban revolutions, the Spanish Civil War, or the 1956 Hungarian Revolt by no means exhausts the list. The ultimate effects of social disasters are probably much greater in terms of population structure than size, not only for the area of occurrence but also in places of refuge.

Political Decisions

Beyond the realm of physical and social disasters, a final group of events molds population patterns—deliberate social, i.e., political, decisions. These decisions are made within the same larger cultural and economic framework that is so critical in deciding population numbers and location. But while the economic and cultural factors discussed previously exert their pressures continuously, ubiquitously, and often quite automatically, the deliberate social decisions are specific, made at given moments for given areas by individuals or small groups of persons. As such, they are subject to the caprices of chance and individual or group psychology, within the limits set by the culture, the economy,

[8] The three major works on such war-induced movements in Europe are in Joseph B. Schechtman, *European Population Transfers, 1939-1945* (New York: Oxford Univ., 1946); Eugene M. Kulischer, *Europe on the Move: War and Population Changes, 1917-1947* (New York: Columbia Univ., 1948); and Malcolm J. Proudfoot, *European Refugees: 1939-1952: A Study in Forced Population Movement* (Evanston: Northwestern Univ., 1956). These and many more publications on the same topic are critically reviewed in Joseph Velikonja, "Postwar Population Movements in Europe," *Annals of the Association of American Geographers,* Vol. 48, No. 4 (December 1958), 458-81.

[9] These migrations are treated in O. H. K. Spate, *India and Pakistan: A General and Regional Geography* (London: Methuen, 1954), pp. 118-21; Irene B. Taeuber, *The Population of Japan* (Princeton: Princeton Univ., 1958), pp. 343-47; and Irene B. Taeuber and George Barclay, "Korea and the Koreans in the Northeast Asian Region," *Population Index,* Vol. 16, No. 3 (October 1950), 229-42. These and other forced shifts in South and East Asia are discussed in International Labour Office, *International Migration, 1945-1957* (Geneva, 1959), pp. 108-31.

and the physical milieu. Thus, quite frequently, many details of the population, large or small, are explicable in terms of decisions that do not neatly fit into any sort of deterministic scheme.

On the national scene, almost all governments zealously regulate the volume and composition of immigration, whether it is temporary or permanent; and often there are even regulations governing the departure of a nation's citizens. Only a few countries have as yet evolved any acknowledged "population policy," but where one does exist, and where it has been implemented, the effects have been palpable. Insofar as the inheritance, ownership, and parceling of land are subject to formal legislation rather than tradition, changes in such laws will have long-lasting reverberations in a country's population patterns. The changing rules governing the disposal of land to individual settlers in the United States, Canada, and other countries of recent heavy immigration have done much to set the pace of colonization and to direct past and present moves.

In addition, a devious, but genuine, relationship exists between the tax policies (almost always pronatal) of many nations and fertility; between national fiscal, trade, labor, and agricultural policy and demographic response; or between international economic agreements of various kinds and the demographic fortunes of certain groups. Changes in prices of gold or sugar, among a number of commodities, by Federal fiat in the United States set off population ripples from the Philippines to the Witwatersrand. The allotment of production quotas for natural rubber or petroleum by quasi-official international consortia have had pronounced, if poorly studied, effects on population movements in the producing areas. Population trends in Ghana cannot be understood without looking into decisions reached on the price of cocoa in the London and New York markets; nor can we understand vital events in Katanga without knowing the price levels for copper and uranium decided, perhaps arbitrarily, in New York and Washington. The instances of population patterns reflecting economic regulation or manipulation are virtually endless.

On a more limited areal scale, governmental agencies have planned, financed, and engineered—not always with complete success—many pioneer colonies. In a centrally planned economy, such as that of China or the Soviet Union, and to a lesser extent in Sweden, Finland, Brazil, Mexico, Canada, and Alaska, the locus of the settlement frontier is sensitive to government edict; but examples can be found in almost any nation that still has some vacant land of moderately good quality. Political decision can also restrict the distribution of specific groups. The greater part of the aboriginal population of the United States and Canada lives on officially designated reservations; in South Africa and Kenya, many Africans are packed into rural "ghettos"; Russian Jews were not permitted outside the western fringes of the Czarist Empire; and during their tenure in the Congo, the Belgians discouraged European settlers from working or residing in most rural areas.

The placement of a military installation in a given locality, often an arbitrary matter, can have startling inflationary effects on the size and structure of the local population. On the other hand, settlement can be greatly inhibited by the establishment of extensive military reservations (for maneuvers or gunnery ranges, for example), or of parks, wilderness areas, and the like. The siting of college campuses, hospitals, penitentiaries, and other institutions having substantial populations can also be subject to private or political whim. Increasingly potent factors in shaping the finer nuances of population distribution are the zoning and planning ordinances coming into force in recent years, not only for urban areas, but for many rural areas as well.

A Summary View

Our initial questions were: why do people live where they do and why are people unevenly distributed over the surface of the earth? We have, by now, established that there is no simple answer for the earth as a whole and that the kind of answer varies greatly from place to place with the circumstances of society, history, and environment. It is also clear that five classes of genetic factors are at work in almost every local situation, always in the matrix of time, and seldom to the exclusion of one another:

(1) direct impact of the physical environment upon human beings
(2) the workings of the economy
(3) general cultural configuration of a society
(4) impact of physical and social disasters
(5) impact of specific social and political decisions

The role of these factors can be briefly summarized: Certain outer limits apparent in the terrestrial environment beyond which human survival, locomotion, and sustenance can be managed only rarely, and then with considerable difficulty, are, specifically, the ocean shore, the edge of ice sheets, the upper boundary of breathable atmosphere, and certain extremely adverse terrains and climates. Within the remaining *ecumene*, it is likely that human work efficiency, pathology, physiological behavior (respiration, digestion, metabolism, reproduction, etc.), and psychological processes are in some measure related to elements in the physical environment or to its totality. The nature and the extent of these relationships remain obscure at this time and can only be elucidated after intensive research. Available evidence does suggest, however, that *direct* environmental influences are relatively unimportant in determining the size, distribution, and structure of populations in those tracts where continuous human residence is feasible.

The nature of the economy—its intrinsic orientation, technology, and stage of development—is critically important in determining which environmental situations can be exploited, how it can be done, and to what degree; thus the economy will strongly influence the number of persons living within a given locality. The economy may also generate its own internal patterning of population numbers and characteristics, with little regard for the physical environment. Through the resource-nexus and the nexus of economic interchange, the economy is generally the most potent immediate factor in determining number, relative spatial disposition, and transfer of people, and is also significant in classifying different kinds of people.

The economic factor is, in turn, controlled by the general cultural configuration of the group, an even broader genetic factor. General cultural traits affect not only economic behavior, but also, in fairly direct fashion, many demographic characteristics, and may operate in ways still too poorly understood to generate certain equilibrial tendencies concerning the size and vital rates of a population. In addition, the size, location, and structure of a group are molded by its specific migratory ethos, its patterns of avoidance or preference for other groups, and other culturally conditioned actions and attitudes. In brief, population size and dynamics are strongly influenced by the automatic operation of the culture; this is also true for the identity and areal aspects of many other demographic characteristics.

Physical and social disasters may spring from causes outside the realm of demography, but their quantitative effects can be profound for limited localities or periods; their qualitative aftermath may be much more prolonged and noteworthy, particularly in the case of social disasters.

Social and political decisions have an incalculably diverse impact on the population map and may be perceptible on any areal scale, from the smallest inhabited tract to the entire planet. Made within the confines of their general and economic cultures, these decisions can influence the channeling of cultural determinants to specific demographic effects. Where the cultural and physical milieus present a variety of options, the choice, as ultimately reflected on the population map, may as often come about through such conscious decision-making as the automatic operation of economy or society.

The variable distribution of human beings over the earth is thus a highly complex phenomenon for which a bewildering assortment of explanations must be offered. In essence, however, all explanations are variations of a single theme that recurs throughout all of human geography: A physically varied, slowly changing planet is occupied by relatively dynamic human groups that are highly diversified in attainments and attitudes. The size and distribution of the population of any given tract is the product of the mutual interplay between society and the physical milieu, and also—to an even greater degree as human groups register new material and social progress—the intragroup and intergroup dealings of residents of this tract. The pertinent equations that link physical, social, and economic determinants with demographic results differ radically from place to place because of changes in physical and cultural conditions, and similarly, they change within the same places with the passage of time. The slow evolution of the habitat, accidents of history, and constant, sometimes abrupt, temporal shifts in socio-economic structure all contribute to constant revisions of the cause-and-effect relationships of population geography. We cannot understand the contemporary population map without an appreciation of the structure, trends, and circumstances of the community for the past several generations, particularly since demographic effects are often not fully realized until long after the generating impulse has vanished. Consequently, time is implicit in considering any of the five broad classes of genetic factors.

This discussion has deliberately centered on population numbers—the simple size and distribution of a group—but the same general approach, using the same five classes of controlling causes, could be equally well applied to almost any significant population trait. We see, then, that the geographer who wishes to explain where people live has taken on a vast, but endlessly interesting, task. Not only must he command locational details for his population, he must also be intimately acquainted with its structure and history. He must wield an encyclopedic knowledge of its physical setting, the minutiae of its economic behavior, the broader lineaments of its cultural and social structure, and virtually all aspects of its human geography, past and present. Furthermore, he must have some insight into the shifting interrelations of all these factors, both as they exist now and as they have been in the past. There is no escaping the thesis that the pursuit of any significant question in population geography inevitably familiarizes the student with every aspect of geography and with many of its neighboring fields.

CHAPTER SEVEN

Interrelations among
demographic traits

Many dimensions and attributes of human populations—other than absolute size—must be described, explained, and interpreted to understand fully the interactions of site, people, and culture that give places their unique geographic personalities. It is not enough simply to explain how and why these population characteristics are as they are. Their reciprocal action upon other geographic phenomena must also be explored to achieve a complete geographic analysis.

If absolute numbers and relative distribution of people have been dealt with in some detail, it was largely for illustrative purposes. Roughly the same sort of analysis could have been applied to any of a dozen or more demographic topics. It does happen that the topic of population size and location appeals to almost everyone, that a relative abundance of information is available on the subject, and that the topic is often a strategic one in that it can lead quickly and effectively to all of the many aspects of population geography.

Any subject as complex as the population geography of a community or area requires identification of the central issues—those on which other elements of the phenomenon seem to be hinged or those so sensitive to the condition of other items as to be particularly valuable for diagnostic purposes. Although population size and distribution most frequently serve this function, they are sometimes less utilitarian than other topics. Population change might well be the central subject for many parts of the contemporary world; ethnic make-up, residential composition, occupational structure, or migrational characteristics might be pivotal elsewhere. A general reconnaissance and an independent, ad hoc selection of the most strategic point of entry are necessary preliminaries to any serious regional study in population geography.

Fortunately, population traits are linked closely to each other. By the nature of the processes that bring them into existence, by certain regularities in the physical and social settings that they occupy, or by the nature of the period in which they occur, they tend to form composite structures with distinct, recurrent patterns. One need only locate the proper key to decode the interconnections among the clusters of traits joined together in these meaningful parcels. Then, starting with any significant biological, social, or dynamic characteristic of a population (although as has been noted, one specific item may be particularly crucial), the investigator can move outward to embrace related topics as he systematically treats the whole spectrum of population geography.

Organic and Other Universal Associations Among Population Traits

What is the nature of the links among population characteristics? Three or four kinds of relationships can be detected.[1] Let us begin with certain organically determined linkages of demographic traits; these are universal and dependent upon basic human biology, with any variations among the races of mankind being either slight or dubious. The risk of death from organic or infectious disease varies greatly with age, achieving a maximum in early infancy, falling off sharply thereafter, and rising gradually after the minimum levels of late childhood and adolescence to the high levels of old age. Such age-specific mortality rates can be observed in any group large enough to minimize the effects of random factors, even though such rates may be obscured occasionally by major epidemics or violent death on a large scale. In addition, a physiologically based sex differential in mortality favors the female during middle and old age (as well as in the fetal period), and a close relationship exists between age or sex on the one hand and cause of death or the risk of incurring any of a long list of maladies on the other. The fecundity of both sexes is, in large part, determined by age; hence, incidence of childbearing is strongly associated with age of parents, modified, of course, by the sexual practices of a given culture and its customary reproductive behavior within or outside of marriage. In all societies a sequence of occupations occurs in the course of the life cycle. Although the identity of this sequence varies widely, its existence is clearly related to changes in the individual's physical and mental capacity that take place during his life span.

Other relationship of population traits are behavioral and presumably

[1] These relationships—their social and economic aspects in particular—are what most concern the demographer. They are dealt with systematically in a good many treatises, among which the following can be especially recommended: United Nations Department of Social Affairs, Population Division, *The Determinants and Consequences of Population Trends: A Summary of the Findings of Studies on the Relationships between Population Changes and Economic and Social Conditions* (New York, 1953); T. Lynn Smith, *Fundamentals of Population Study* (Philadelphia: Lippincott, 1960); William Petersen, *Population* (New York: Macmillan, 1961).

cultural in origin, but are so widespread that they are taken for granted. In fact, much of the behavior in question might be instinctive as much as learned. For instance, the nature of the tasks pursued by males may vary radically from those performed by females. Childbearing is perhaps the only indisputably female chore, but males have had almost exclusive control over warfare, the more hazardous kinds of hunting, and other aggressive activities calling for decided physical prowess. Almost all given tasks are emphatically described as male or female, although there are certain occupations that may be allotted to either sex, depending on the mores of a given society. The family (with or without formal marriage) is another universal phenomenon; it serves as the basic social, sexual, reproductive, educational, and until recently, economic unit of a society. The absence of normal family organization or the normal balance of the sexes—situations found in raw frontier societies, institutional populations, or certain violently disturbed groups—will occasion low fertility, a distorted age structure, and rather extreme occupational and migrational conditions.

Although the foregoing relationships are basic, important, and universal, they are rivaled (and generally exceeded) in significance and far outnumbered by the correlations among demographic traits specific to given societies. Certain types of individual relationships may be repeated with little change from place to place, but taken as a whole, they are unique for a given area or people. Obviously, a great many relationships are completely missing among the less technologically advanced societies because the necessary characteristics simply do not exist. Society is relatively uncomplicated where people subsist by hunting and gathering or where they operate at the more rudimentary stages of agricultural development. Cities do not exist in these societies, hence, the population is not split into urban and rural components. Neither writing nor formal education has developed, so the distinctions of education or literacy are not present. Only a faint suggestion of social classes or occupational specialization is evident—except for those established by sex and age. Monetary income has little, if any, meaning, and there are no meaningful distinctions in standard of living or housing conditions. Each of these groups is normally racially homogeneous, and all members speak the same language and hold the same religious beliefs (both the language and the religion may be limited to the group in question). Even though the community as a whole may shift from one place to another, virtually no individuals or families migrate into or out of the community, hence there is no migration in a social sense—except for the war captives or brides taken from neighboring communities.

Correlations of Residential Status with Population Composition

A more complex society, developing from technological advances, expands the roster of categories into which a population can be classified, and vastly amplifies associations among these categories. All such linkages can be grouped into two large classes: the basically logical and functional, and the random or arbitrary. Among the former, four major groups of associations, namely those based on residence, migratory status, class, and occupation, can be detected in relatively advanced societies. These exist in addition to the universal, organic linkages already discussed (age-mortality, sex-mortality, age- and sex-morbidity, age-fertility, and age-occupation), but may frequently be entangled with them.

Residential status is the basis for what is perhaps the most striking system of trait associations. Groups change as they evolve from emphatically rural, isolated communities to rural populations that are increasingly exposed to metropolitan influences, through villages of increasing size and complexity, up the ranks of small and medium cities to the largest conurbations. Aside from a great increase in population density, one immediately notices an increasing complexity of function and, thus, of occupational structure; greater diversity of racial and ethnic stocks, language, and religion than is usually found in small country villages becomes visible as the cities grow. Average income and standard of living tend to be distinctly higher in cities than in rural areas, but deviations from the norm also tend to be much wider. The class structure of the city diverges greatly from that of rural areas but it usually does so in ways that apply only to a given region. Urban populations are very different from rural groups in terms of age and sex composition; generally there is a stronger representation of young adults and an imbalance of the sexes. Almost everywhere, urban fertility and family size have been significantly below rural levels, sometimes very much so; and the mobility of city folk has been disproportionately high as metropolises grow largely by migration from the countryside and from other cities. Levels of mortality, patterns of morbidity, marital structures, and causes of death are different in cities and rural areas, but because they vary through time and from place to place, broad generalizations are impossible. Cities have, as a class, registered much stronger positive rates of net growth than have rural tracts; and the larger the city the greater, generally, the absolute and relative increase.

Virtually every index of socioeconomic achievement measures cities well ahead of the countryside: literacy, educational attainment, or percentage of labor force in the professions and other relatively advanced occupations. Whether or not urban areas are superior in the realm of housing is less clear-cut, but there are sharp differences in kind between urban and rural housing in every society, the direction and nature of these differences again varying greatly from place to place. For any urbanized nation, a system of internal differentiation within individual cities can also be postulated, particularly in larger metropolises; we can make distinct associations between traits on the one hand and city neighborhoods, in terms of age, function, or location, on the other. However, the ground rules for such a demographic anatomy of cities diverge considerably among different urban cultures, making it hopeless to look for any valid generalizations here.

Functional Associations Among Other Population Traits: Migration, Class, and Occupation

Other functionally related traits surround the phenomenon of migration, where a population with a strong complement of relatively recent in-migrants is likely to differ radically from one that has surrendered a large number.[2] Contrasts between migrant and residual groups can run the full gamut of demographic characteristics, but the nature of such contrasts depends on the specific kind of move in question, making broad generalizations dangerous. In each case, the volume of migration as well as its date, duration, source, distance, motivation, degree of freedom, and other factors must all be weighed before one can establish relationships between migration and population structure. Once the necessary groundwork has been completed, such an analysis could supply powerful insights into the population geography of either migrant or residual societies.

The two foregoing types of associations are especially appealing to geographers because they are so often expressed in areal terms. Several very important parts of the world stand out boldly on the population map because of their overwhelmingly metropolitan character (see Map 2), e.g., the great urban-industrial belt stretching east-southeast across Europe from Belgium to the central Ukraine, the English Midlands, the northeastern United States and the southeastern fringe of Canada, the hive of cities in northern Italy, or the large and medium centers in southern Honshu.[3] Equally prominent are those broad zones that are decidedly rural in character; but even where rural and urban populations are closely intermingled, one can usually regionalize a population on the basis of residence, and fruitfully pursue spatial contrasts of urban and rural areas in population structure without too much difficulty. Similarly, it is feasible to mark off zones of strong, persistent in-migration from those serving as human reservoirs and to detect significant geographic differences in their populations. Needless to say, there is considerable, though incomplete, overlap in the identity of peoples and places classified according to the urban-rural and migratory scales.

---

[2] Unfortunately, no suitable terminology has been devised for such antithetic populations or areas; for the moment, they will be labeled "migrant" and "residual," respectively.

[3] Considering the importance of the phenomenon, it is remarkable that so little has been published on world patterns of urbanization. Perhaps the most useful items are in Kingsley Davis and Hilda Hertz, "The World Distribution of Urbanization," *Bulletin of the International Statistical Institute*, Vol. 33, No. 4 (1954), 227-43; Norton Ginsburg, "Urban Population," in *Atlas of Economic Development* (Chicago: Univ. of Chicago, 1961), pp. 34-37; Homer Hoyt, *World Urbanization: Expanding Population in a Shrinking World*, Urban Land Institute, Technical Bulletin No. 43 (Washington, 1962), and "World Urbanism," *The American Journal of Sociology*, Vol. 40, No. 5 (March 1955).

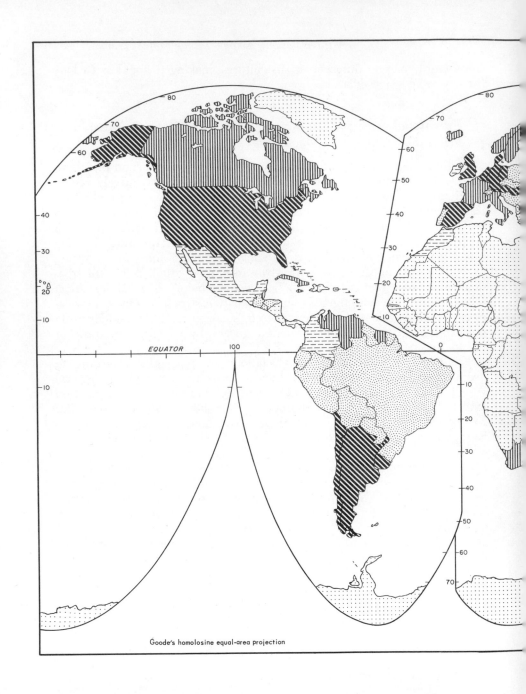

Goode's homolosine equal-area projection

2. Levels of Urbanization.

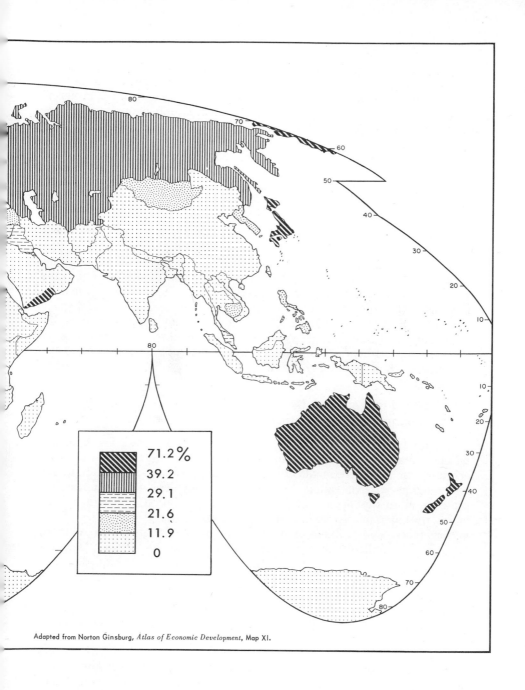

Percentage of Population in 20,000+ Cities, ca. 1958

Adapted from Norton Ginsburg, *Atlas of Economic Development*, Map XI.

Legend:

	71.2 %
	39.2
	29.1
	21.6
	11.9
	0

The remaining functional associations of traits are not so immediately important to geographers, though they are very interesting to the demographer. Social class and economic standing, whether defined in terms of income, power, or prestige, carry with them strong demographic concomitants with major variations from culture to culture. Generally, the higher a man is in society, the greater is the likelihood of low mortality and fertility, a high degree of spatial mobility, urban residence, and superior housing facilities; his morbidity pattern is quite distinct from that of the people beneath him, he is usually literate, has had a prolonged period of schooling, and holds one of the more skilled or prestigious jobs.

Even though it is not feasible to rank all occupations in strict linear fashion, from lowest to highest (who rates higher, a farmer or a tool-and-die maker?), it is certainly true that every major occupation or industry carries with it distinctive demographic consequences. The traits associated with either class or occupation tend to be stratified primarily in social space; and it is seldom that their areal sorting in physical space is more than dimly discernible. Since their spatial expression is indistinct and often smothered by other genetic factors more sensitive to location, geographers are only marginally concerned with class and occupation in their population studies.

Race, Language, and Religion as Demographic Determinants

Other functional associations among population traits are centered on race, language, religion, and to some extent, sex, and these are random, arbitrary, or even irrational. Overt differences among races, languages, and religions are, of course, obvious, but many less visible differences are even more significant. Intensive research has failed, however, to disclose any inherent distinctions in the mental or moral capacities of the various races. The problem of superior vs. inferior languages or religions is much more difficult. One language may better express certain concepts than another, or a given religion may be hypertrophic in one direction and stunted in another. Judging the relative excellence of a language or a theology in its entirety is, however, subject to personal opinion. In any case, certain races, languages, and religions have achieved higher status than others through historical chance rather than because of innate superiority or inferiority.

As an example, take contemporary British East Africa, where the population has been rigidly stratified along racial lines that also divide languages, religions, and classes. The lower strata of society are composed of native Africans who speak various Bantu and Sudanic languages and observe their traditional tribal religions, except for a Christianized minority. At a somewhat higher level, a much smaller group of East Indians, mainly Hindu in religion, still speak their original languages. At the highest level, a small European minority professes Christianity and speaks English. The demographic structure of each of the three racial communities is distinctive, and insofar as population characteristics can be rated quantitatively, they parallel racial-social status.

Among an infinite number of planets that might have physical conditions similar to those of the earth, and on which human life might have evolved, it is possible to imagine a region on one such planet where a society similar to that of British East Africa has arisen. It is also conceivable that such a society might have a small Negro upper class speaking Bantu and adhering to Hinduism or some esoteric African cult, while the lowly masses might be white- or brown-skinned Christian Caucasians speaking English. Although this would be the inverse of the present East African society, very much the same kinds of traits that we noted earlier would be associated with residence, migratory status, class, and occupation. In any case, one can observe in many parts of the world important groups of demographic traits that are intimately involved with race, language, and religion. Because these associations often have distinct areal patterns, they can be of great concern to the geographer and should be sought out and fully exploited by him.

An Approach to a Geographic Typology of Population Regions

It is well to recall here the ultimate objective of population geography: to understand the variable population traits of places, their causes, consequences, and above all, their interactions with other physical and cultural elements, thereby producing a distinct geographic personality for each inhabited part of the earth. Two possible approaches to this goal have been examined—analyzing the distributional patterns of a series of important population characteristics, and studying the spatial covariation of diverse sets of genetically linked traits.

Although these two techniques are useful, there is still need for a more comprehensive framework within which these and other methods can be manipulated for optimum results—one within which the highest level of discourse, genuine geographic analysis, is attainable. Such a broad methodological framework should give the student a vivid, immediate sense of the location in space and time of the phenomena under scrutiny. If a small part of a country is being examined, the interconnections between its population and that of the entire nation should be readily visible; and if a nation is being scrutinized, an ideal methodology would clearly illuminate the similarities and differences of its population against those of other nations. A satisfactory methodology must tie the microregion to the macroregion and the latter to the world, and it must give us tempo designations showing the direction and rates of change. Above all, it must point the way to both the broadest and the deepest geographical interpretation of population facts.

This is expecting a great deal of any methodology. What is offered here is, frankly, an experimental model that presupposes knowledge we may not have at our disposal for a good many years, although some current research trends have indicated that much of the missing material may be produced in the not too distant future. In keeping with the complexity of the reality it seeks to explore, this system offers no simple formulas that can be used without considerable preparatory work. Equally disquieting to those who visualize the world in terms of reiterative patterns is the discovery that each region delineated by this system is sui generis, and that only in a limited fashion does it duplicate the features of other regions.

The proposed scheme applies to the study of either regions (from the smallest locality to the largest nations) or given ethnic groups or other coherent populations, including some that may be noncontiguous in distribution. The population geographies of the Finns or the Chinese would be distinctly different from those of either Finland or China, even though such studies would share much common ground. Both approaches are, of course, valid; the choice depends upon research objectives. In order to avoid needless repetition, it should be understood that when the terms "area," "region," or a synonym appear, one may also read "population," "folk," "ethnic group," or an equivalent term. The proposed typology yields a classification of areas that is useful not only for population geography but also for other branches of cultural and economic geography.

CHAPTER EIGHT

A cultural approach to the regionalization of populations

The Primacy of the Cultural Factor

In trying to find a rationale for mankind's uneven distribution over the earth, we have seen that within inhabited tracts the direct influence of the physical environment is rather slight, the impact of physical disasters is seldom either widespread or long-lasting, and the major determinants of the size and distribution of a population are essentially cultural in nature—the structure of the economy, the general cultural configuration of the society, various social disasters, and specific social and political decisions. Within a given physical context, population size and structure are the products of the internal workings of a cultural system and of its interactions with other systems elsewhere. This notion can be corroborated, as has been pointed out above, by studying the covariance of clusters of demographic traits. In some cases, the general pattern of such associations is universal but the details are governed by the nature of the particular culture. In other instances, the entire pattern of covariance is quite specific to the individual culture. The conclusion is obvious: *The first and most important step in approaching the population geography of an area is to identify and characterize its basic cultural patterns, and more specifically, to probe the demographic implications of these patterns.*[1]

[1] This simple, but evidently original statement is at odds with a great deal of geographic and demographic literature, but the intrinsic logic of the argument and the evidence that can be adduced from many parts of the world seem compelling reasons for setting forth such an axiom. The real problem would appear to be not whether the axiom is valid, but why social scientists have been so reluctant to recognize the importance of the cultural factor in population phenomena.

Unfortunately, this is much more easily said than done. Despite much interest on the parts of anthropogeographers and anthropologists, little consensus has been reached either on the methods to be used or the results thus far obtained in identifying and mapping culture areas. Furthermore, there is a severe shortage of reliable information on the demographic connotations of different cultures. The population phenomena of Europe and North America, whose cultures are fairly similar, have been diverse and interesting enough to absorb almost all the energies of demographers, yet these phenomena have not fostered a keen appreciation of the importance of cultural attitudes as variables in demographic equations. Although major attention has been directed toward non-European peoples only recently, good academic and practical reasons indicate that we may expect a surge of interest in such studies in the immediate future. This broadening of the demographic field may well bring about a more complete knowledge of the demographic axioms of a variety of cultures. In the meantime, we must rely on fragmentary data or indirect inferences for the cultural determinants of demographic behavior for most of the world.

The Identity of Culture Areas

Accepting the primacy of the cultural element in any methodology does involve difficulties in identifying or limiting culture areas. The population geographer must exploit such materials as may be on hand, and patiently await the new findings that can be reasonably anticipated. The magnitude, complexity, and poorly understood inner workings of cultural phenomena all conspire to make delimiting valid culture areas a risky business.[2]

Cultural systems comprise that huge mass of *learned* behavior, attitudes, and ideas that control the greater part of their participants' thoughts and actions. The possible combinations of characteristics are so numerous that no two individuals are culturally identical; indeed, each constitutes a kind of cultural microregion. At the other extreme, certain cultural practices are almost universal—the use of language and of fire, the tabu against incest, the possession of domesticated dogs; relying on such criteria, the entire human species might be regarded as sharing a cultural macroregion. Actually, of course, certain intermediate cultural units, ranging in size from single villages to regions of subcontinental expanse, are operatively of much more importance. These are identified as groups of people regarded as "belonging together," having a common heritage, or being more like one another than like other folk, either by themselves or by other groups.

[2] For a series of thoughtful essays on various aspects of the distribution and regionalization of cultural traits, and for valuable references to other studies, see "Cultural Areas and Distributions," Part II, particularly the "Introduction," in Philip L. Wagner and Marvin W. Mikesell, eds., *Readings in Cultural Geography* (Chicago: Univ. of Chicago, 1962), pp. 55-201.

This sense of identity is most powerful at the lower strata and becomes increasingly diffuse as the culture area grows larger and more inclusive. A Bavarian peasant would have a strong sense of solidarity with his fellow villagers, a somewhat weaker, but still potent, feeling for other villages in his *gemeinde,* or district, and a still more dilute, though quite definite affinity for all other Bavarians. Pressed sufficiently hard, he would confess to a distant relationship to Prussians, Saxons, Austrians, and other rather alien Teutons. But unless he were highly educated, our Bavarian would fail to recognize his membership in an extended cultural clan of Scottish Highlanders or Polish peasants, even though they all speak cognate languages, profess the same religion, have much the same somatic characteristics, and basically similar material cultures. (A visit to an utterly alien people like the Papuans might, however, make him more responsive to pan-European resemblances upon his return.) At national or primary subnational levels in particular, "ethnic group" is applicable to the relatively homogeneous cultural group; but for our purposes, the more inclusive terms "cultural group" and "culture area" are more useful.

What traits reveal a sense of cultural solidarity? Which of them can be used for identification purposes, even when direct evidence of group sentiment is lacking? A few traits are particularly valuable for diagnostic purposes, but race is emphatically not one of these—except for groups that have been isolated for long periods, such as the Bushmen of South Africa, the Australian aborigines, the Lapps, or the Ainu of the Kurile Islands and Hokkaido, or where it reinforces the existence of subcultures, as among the American Negro, the Cape Coloured, or some of the Hindu castes. Normally, appreciable physical diversity can be expected within any except the smallest of culture areas; and in extreme cases, such as Brazil or Puerto Rico, there may be a kaleidoscopic mixture of racial stocks. The economic aspects of a culture are much more useful than race, if one recognizes that any given basic economic pattern may be common to several groups and that its subtler variations must be used to segregate the various entities. The same observation applies to religion, costume, diet, architecture and other artifacts, settlement patterns, folklore, art, and social organization—all quite serviceable traits when used with caution.

Language as the Prime Criterion of Culture

The most universal and most subtle indicator of culture is, by common agreement, language.[3] There are many ways to establish that this is so, but the strong emotion each speaker feels for his language is evidence enough. The particular structure and flavor of a language, or dialect, is closely intertwined with the culture; if one is a member of

---

[3] For a brief, general introduction to the subject see C. M. Delgado de Carvalho, "The Geography of Languages," pp. 75-93, and also the editors' discussion, in Philip L. Wagner and Marvin W. Mikesell, eds., *Readings in Cultural Geography,* pp. 56-57.

that culture, he will inevitably speak and think in its language. It is also recognized, both by laymen and social scientists, that the acculturation of one group by another will take place when the language of the dominant group is adopted—hence the fierceness of the struggle either to suppress or sustain the tongue of beleaguered minorities. To the extent that approximate linguistic uniformity is found over broad expanses— for example, English in Anglo-America, Russian over much of the Soviet Union, and Spanish in the greater part of Latin America—we have confirming evidence of the general cultural cohesiveness of these huge areas that are at the top level of the hierarchy of culture areas.

Normally, however, language gaps of varying degrees of impermeability are found at the lower provincial or tribal level. Local dialects, such as those that abound in Great Britain and are less numerous, but still perceptible, in the United States, may indicate emergent or relict culture areas. Where these dialects reach the limits of mutual intelligibility—as happens within Spain, Italy, and portions of France—one finds culture areas of an intermediate order. In other cases, a common language has evolved within the limits of a higher-order culture area, giving rise to an entire family of distinct languages. China, for instance, has a common written language but several spoken languages that are not ordinarily mutually understandable. Quite frequently, in medium- or higher-order culture areas, such as those depicted in Map 3, one may find many distantly related languages as well as others that are totally alien to one another. In fact, the Caucasus, New Guinea and other portions of Melanesia, pre-Columbian California, and the uplands of Southeast Asia, areas regarded as distinct higher-order culture regions by many anthropologists, are veritable Towers of Babel.

Since the evolutionary career of culture in general and language in particular need not necessarily coincide, one must be wary of generalizations. The French are culturally bound more closely to the Germans, or to the Basques, who speak a totally unrelated tongue, than they are to the citizens of Haiti or Guadeloupe, who speak a French patois. Jamaica is, after a fashion, English-speaking, but there are only weak ties between that island and Great Britain. A modern, Antillean cultural community has developed during the past three centuries under the deep social shock of plantation slavery and its aftermath. It is in this community that Jamaica shares membership with the Haitians, the Guadeloupéennes, and other dominantly Negroid folk who may speak not only variants of French and English, but also Spanish, Dutch, Danish, or some local hybrid tongue. The patterns of mating, fertility, morbidity, mortality, land-use and settlement forms, and migration within this Antillean system are distinct not only from the mother countries but from all other nonplantation regions as well. So we see that although language is the best single criterion for detecting culture areas, it attains maximum effectiveness only on the lower rungs of the hierarchical ladder of cultures. At higher levels, it must be applied with considerable caution.

The National State as a Culture Area

The relationship of the nation to the culture area presents a problem that is difficult to resolve.[4] Where national boundaries have been drawn in clear cognizance of ethnic realities, or where isolation or intense reaction between a government and the governed is the rule, national territory and culture area are synonymous. Japan, Korea, the Malagasy Republic, Albania, Iceland, Israel, or Haiti, and with major reservations, Eire, Hungary, Indonesia, or the Philippines are examples. Many other single nations exist as plural, or at least diverse, societies, in which several distinct cultures show some degree of territorial segregation; and quite often a given culture area may be divided among two or more nations. However, given enough time, stability, and nationalistic pressure, international boundaries may eventually mark distinct discontinuities within once homogeneous culture areas. The alert observer can note interesting shades of difference in speech, social psychology, settlement forms, and other cultural features on both sides of the unusually permeable United States-Canadian border (even though such differences are slight as compared with the similarities in this major culture area). Sharp differences appeared between those portions of Poland that were separated by the German-Russian border until 1918; but here also the essential integrity of the Polish culture area remained intact. This problem of imperfect identity between nation and culture area is an especially poignant one for the geographer, since population data are ordinarily available in national packages or are expressed in the variable statistical idioms of different nations.

The student must avoid the easy assumption that nationality and cultural identity coincide; if his subject area is the entire nation, he must diligently scout for whatever subnational or international culture areas may be present and learn what he can about their demographic connotations. Even in a nation like the United States, where the cliché of a homogenized mass culture is widespread, cultural discontinuities still exist. Leaving aside recent, unassimilated immigrants—notably French Canadians, Puerto Ricans, and Mexicans—we find that the culture of the American South, especially its Negro and white southern Appalachian components, the Mormon region of the Great Basin, and several smaller tracts where certain pietistic sects are solidly entrenched, deviates sufficiently from national demographic norms to call for special treatment.

[4] Political geographers have been greatly concerned with the relationship of nationality to culture, and particularly language, but usually in specific regional contexts. This is, perhaps, best exemplified in Leon Dominian, *The Frontiers of Language and Nationality in Europe* (New York: American Geographical Soc., 1917). For explicit statements of the role of culture in the life of the national state see H. W. Weigert, et al., *Principles of Political Geography* (New York: Appleton, 1957), pp. 293-445, and Samuel Van Valkenburg and Carl L. Stotz, *Elements of Political Geography*, 2nd ed. (Englewood Cliffs: Prentice-Hall, 1954), pp. 247-303.

A World Map of Culture Areas

In general, then, the larger the culture area, the less useful language is as a diagnostic tool (along with other more or less localized nonmaterial elements); it is replaced by various phases of social and political organization, the economic system, and certain elements of material culture in the identification of culture areas. Usually, locating and classifying culture areas of limited tract is quite difficult and almost unmanageable if attempted on a uniform basis for the entire world. The geographer must almost always accept available expert opinion, but occasionally, if he has the necessary raw materials and skills, he can himself demarcate those cultures that may have demographic significance.

The areas adopted from Spencer and Johnson's *Atlas for Anthropology* (see Map 3) represent the only known published effort to map culture areas for the entire world with any degree of precision; they are offered chiefly to suggest the kinds of higher-order areas the geographer might confront. They are in no sense definitive, and many of the boundaries are, in fact, quite controversial. A date has been omitted deliberately to show the disposition of culture areas before the impact of expanding European cultures or other recent, relatively advanced civilizations. The date is "contact time" for those peoples whose culture, or very existence, was shattered by Europeanization, and is the present period for those with greater powers of resistance; the date varies, then, from 1492 for the Caribbean, to the twentieth century for most of Africa and Asia. Why has no one tried to update the map? The extraordinary character of the past four and one-half centuries gives the answer: An explosive technological and scientific revolution emanated from Western Europe, profoundly affecting geography as well as modern history. Almost as important has been the large-scale dispersal of the Europeans themselves.

The Europeanization of the World

In 1500, on the eve of this great social upheaval, the territorial identity of culture areas was relatively clear-cut—only "relatively" so because zones of change and transition were common as the age-old processes of internal evolution, foreign conquest, and diffusion of traits ceaselessly continued their work. European people, with their techniques and ideas, have, however, introduced new dimensions to the cultural compartmentalization of the world. In a number of places, European colonists simply annihilated, thrust aside, or otherwise crushed to a state of impotence pre-existing peoples and cultures. But more frequently, the newcomers only partially replaced the indigenous population, and "modern" methods and notions were selectively introduced. Quite often European elements were superimposed on earlier ones without a complete merger. It is important to know that this was a universal phenomenon. The trans-

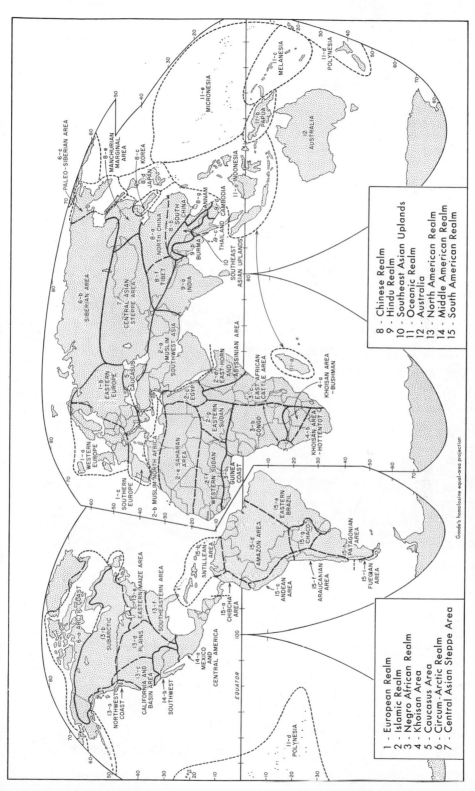

3. Generalized Culture Areas and Realms, as of Contact Time (A.D. 1500 to Present)

1 - European Realm
2 - Islamic Realm
3 - Negro African Realm
4 - Khoisan Realm
5 - Caucasus Area
6 - Circum-Arctic Realm
7 - Central Asian Steppe Area

8 - Chinese Realm
9 - Hindu Realm
10 - Southeast Asian Uplands
11 - Oceanic Realm
12 - Australia
13 - North American Realm
14 - Middle American Realm
15 - South American Realm

Goode's homolosine equal-area projection

71

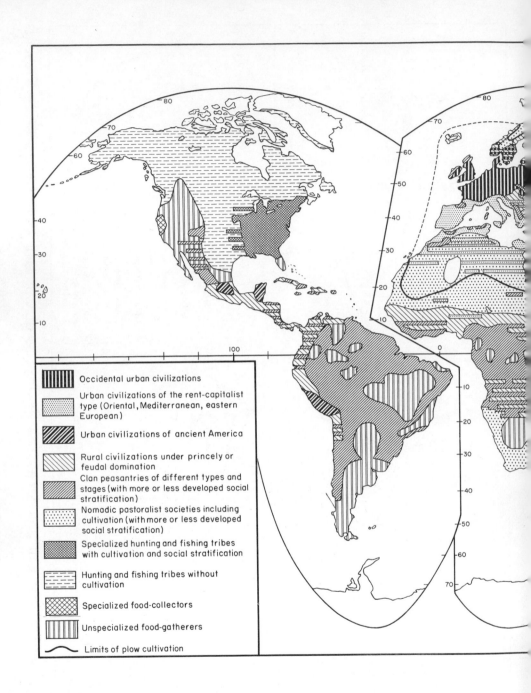

Occidental urban civilizations

Urban civilizations of the rent-capitalist type (Oriental, Mediterranean, eastern European)

Urban civilizations of ancient America

Rural civilizations under princely or feudal domination

Clan peasantries of different types and stages (with more or less developed social stratification)

Nomadic pastoralist societies including cultivation (with more or less developed social stratification)

Specialized hunting and fishing tribes with cultivation and social stratification

Hunting and fishing tribes without cultivation

Specialized food-collectors

Unspecialized food-gatherers

Limits of plow cultivation

4. Stages of Socioeconomic Evolution

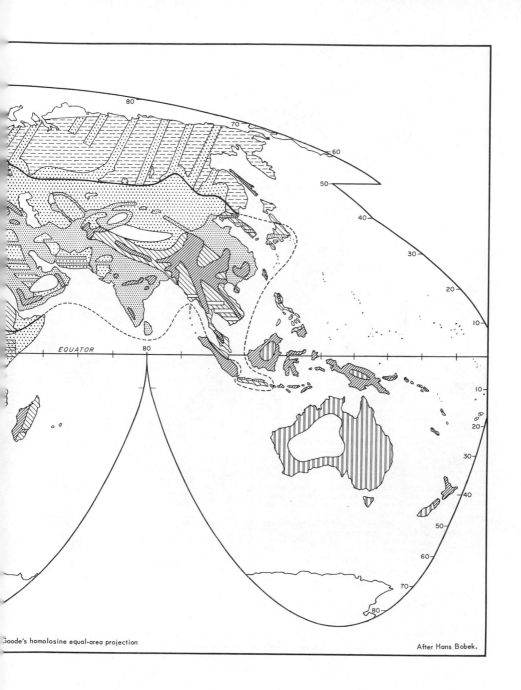

Goode's homolosine equal-area projection

After Hans Bobek.

at the End of the Fifteenth Century

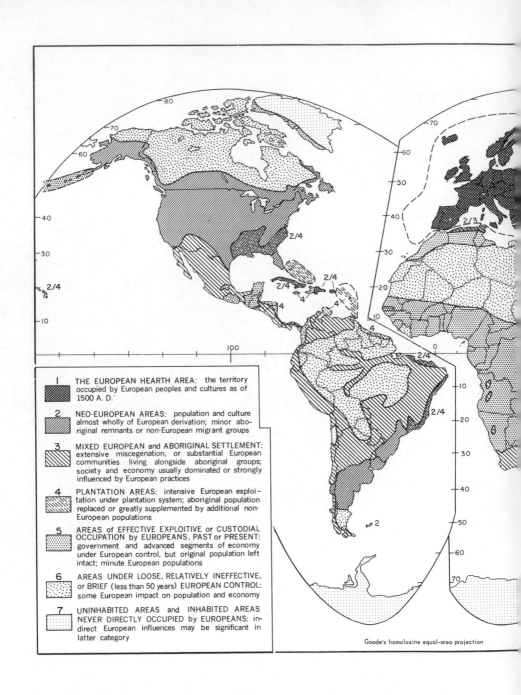

1 THE EUROPEAN HEARTH AREA: the territory occupied by European peoples and cultures as of 1500 A.D.

2 NEO-EUROPEAN AREAS: population and culture almost wholly of European derivation; minor aboriginal remnants or non-European migrant groups

3 MIXED EUROPEAN and ABORIGINAL SETTLEMENT: extensive miscegenation, or substantial European communities living alongside aboriginal groups; society and economy usually dominated or strongly influenced by European practices

4 PLANTATION AREAS: intensive European exploitation under plantation system; aboriginal population replaced or greatly supplemented by additional non-European populations

5 AREAS of EFFECTIVE EXPLOITIVE or CUSTODIAL OCCUPATION by EUROPEANS, PAST or PRESENT: government and advanced segments of economy under European control, but original population left intact; minute European populations

6 AREAS UNDER LOOSE, RELATIVELY INEFFECTIVE, or BRIEF (less than 50 years) EUROPEAN CONTROL: some European impact on population and economy

7 UNINHABITED AREAS and INHABITED AREAS NEVER DIRECTLY OCCUPIED by EUROPEANS: indirect European influences may be significant in latter category

Goode's homolosine equal-area projection

5. The Europeanization of the World

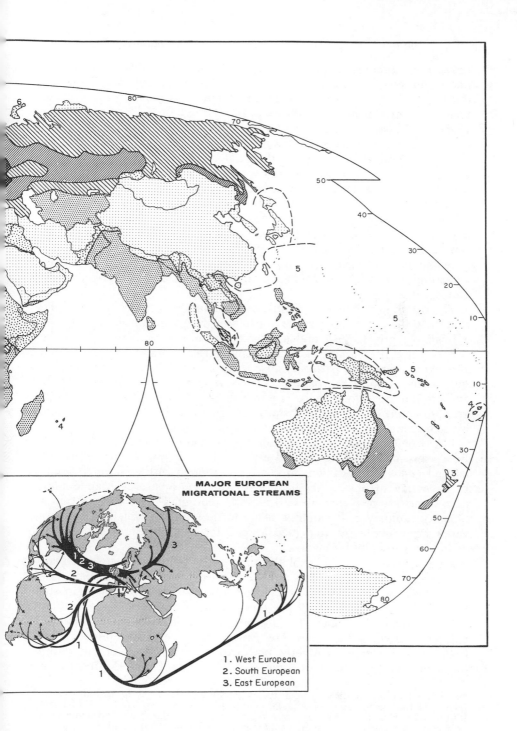

MAJOR EUROPEAN MIGRATIONAL STREAMS

1. West European
2. South European
3. East European

ference of European migrants to "new" lands was widespread, though not unlimited (see Map 5). In much of the remaining non-European territory, European powers wielded political hegemony for various lengths of time—from over 400 years for Portuguese Africa to a bare 5 years for Italian Ethiopia. Europeans failed to penetrate only where extreme military inaccessibility was a factor. Tibet, Nepal, Afghanistan, Ethiopia (until 1935), most of the Arabian Peninsula, and Japan are examples. The mutual suspicions of would-be conquerors also forestalled action in countries such as China, Siam, Iran, or Turkey. But even there, as in all parts of the non-European world, a variable, yet important, infusion of European travelers, goods, techniques, religious cults, plants and animals, and other cultural merchandise took place. By 1945, European influences had reached even the most distant, isolated groups, with the possible exception of some small tribes hidden in the least accessible corners of the Amazon and Orinoco basins or highland New Guinea.

The resulting mélange of multilevel (or plural) societies is something quite new in human history, as are those groups in transition between a relatively private past and a dynamic future in which they will be part of a highly complex, planetary community. A single drawing cannot adequately show this, partly because there is not enough recent material, but mostly because the patterns vary vertically as well as horizontally and are too intricate to map. The reader is invited to work out a rough approximation of the cultural status of any area that may concern him by comparing three or four of the accompanying maps.

Places within the heart of Europe or those places within which Europeans have fully supplanted earlier folk (see Map 5), can safely be labeled genus Europeanicus in character, though further inquiry would be necessary to determine the precise species. Wherever Map 5 indicates a mixture of European settlers with aboriginal population, a transitional or multilayered society is likely to be found in which the culture varies horizontally by area (see Map 3 for the non-European components) or vertically by class.

Algeria, from the middle of the nineteenth century when large-scale European immigration began until the end of French rule in 1962, is a good illustration of such mixed regions.[5] Although the Europeans (mostly French) made up only about one-tenth of the country's total population, they effectively controlled its government and economy, and generally enjoyed a privileged position. The Europeans were concentrated mainly in the coastal sections of Algeria, both within the larger cities and within the superior agricultural districts (78 per cent of the Europeans, as

---

[5] The best recent discussion of the country's population is in Dorothy Good, "Notes on the Demography of Algeria," *Population Index*, Vol. 27, No. 1 (January 1961), 3-32. For discussions of other regions of mixed European and indigenous population, see Lawrence Krader, *Peoples of Central Asia*, Uralic and Altaic series, Vol. 26 (Bloomington: Indiana Univ., 1962); John H. Wellington, *Southern Africa: A Geographical Study*, Vol. 2 (Cambridge: Cambridge Univ., 1955), pp. 201-70; and Monica M. Cole, *South Africa* (London: Methuen, 1961), pp. 653-67.

against 19 per cent of the Moslems, were reported as urban in 1954). Strict areal segregation was observed within the cities. Both demographically and economically, the two groups were dissimilar. Only 29.2 per cent of the European labor force was engaged in agriculture in 1954, as opposed to 74.5 per cent of the Moslem group, but production per unit (and per capita income) was much higher for the Europeans, so that they provided most of the marketable farm produce. The disproportion in per capita income, if figures were available, would probably be even greater within the nonagricultural section of the economy. The Moslem fertility rate was more than twice that of the European—a crude birth rate of 52.4 in 1959 as against the European 22.0. Death rates were similarly divergent—20.7 as compared to 9.3—and the ratio of infant mortality was on the order of 5 to 1. Virtually all of the European community was literate, but 86 per cent of Moslem males, 6 years and older, and 95 per cent of the females were reported as illiterate in 1954. Similar differentials could be cited for many other aspects of demography and the economy, but the conclusion is obvious: Pre-existing intercultural differences have been preserved, and even reinforced by the areal separation and class stratification of the two groups.

In areas such as Algeria, or where European influences have been less direct, one can gauge the degree to which the traditional culture (see Map 3) has been modernized and an alien stratum superimposed by comparing Map 4, "The Stages of Socioeconomic Development as of A.D. 1500," with Map 6, in which the current level of economic development has been sketched. Though badly distorted and radically changed, many premodern culture areas still exist in places where European penetration has been less aggressive. Where the invaders did not demolish indigenous cultures they often helped to "freeze" them in their momentary locations. A few shifts in cultural boundaries, such as the southward push of Islam in West Africa, were uninterrupted by the European presence; but much more often the migrations, conquests, and other wholesale changes that would normally have occurred were intercepted by the new governors and the *status quo* was upheld.

The Ranking of Cultures

Whether or not cultures can be given relative, qualitative ratings is a problem that reaches far down into the philosophical underpinnings of anthropology and cultural geography. To say that the problem is being solved daily through brute military and economic force, that the most technically virtuosic are surviving and the technically unskilled are perishing is easy enough, but such an approach obviously oversimplifies a complex situation. In the pecuniary world of today, economic innovation or progress reaps almost instantaneous material wealth. The factors of survival and immediate selfish gain are so powerful in forming contemporary population patterns that they are basic elements in the methodology offered here. If political and technological prowess were taken as the sole criteria, rating societies in terms of an appropriate socioeconomic scale would not be difficult.

But cultures have other aspects of equal or greater intrinsic worth, though of little relevance to economic or military matters; and specifically, their aesthetic, ethical, and ecological values may be very important. Many cultures have excelled all others in one or more branches of human thought or endeavor, even though they were later overcome by superior military forces or economic technologies. The Roman conquest of Greece, the Turkish sweep over the remnants of the Byzantine Empire, the Mongol invasion of thirteenth-century China, or the Spanish plundering of Mexico and Peru are all examples of this. Even if we exclude all but the strictly material factors, which culture must we judge to be superior—the one that persists in sensitive balance with its environing resources or the one that extracts the maximum wealth in the shortest time from these resources with no thought of the future? On an ecological scale, the Bushmen of the Kalahari far outrank the Europeans who cannot exist there without aid from the outside; and no one has been able to find much use for Baja California since its aboriginal culture was extinguished.

We must also reckon with the historical dimension. Few citizens of Northwest Europe would hesitate to proclaim that their culture is superior in every respect to the Islamic culture; but 1,000 years ago, even though both cultures were essentially the same as they are today, any objective critic would have emphatically stated that the Islamic was superior to the European culture. Actually, no satisfactory way of ranking cultures is known at this time. Because cultures are different, it is fair to compare them only with respect to those specific topics and periods for which relative status can be objectively scored.

The Cultural Approach: A Summary

When the geographer has fully defined the culture of an area (and has inventoried its physical geography), he has all the background material needed to analyze the population geography of that area. Classifying areas by economy, political structure, or physical region yields a valuable, but limited, set of facts and probabilities about their populations. However, once the total structure, rhythm, and "style" of the culture is grasped, everything is found to be implict in it—economic and social structure, ecological responses to the environment, and the more likely reactions to a variety of shifting circumstances. The indispensability of the cultural approach was forcefully illustrated by the "baby boom" that took place in the United States during the 1940's and 1950's. This utterly unforeseen, immensely important change in fertility pattern would seem to indicate a shallow understanding by population scientists of the basic nature of the American cultural psyche and/or basic changes in American culture brought about by the impact of new social and economic conditions.

The first step, then, for the geographer studying an area's population is to establish its cultural identity and to reconnoiter the demographic and geographic implications of this identity. The procedure can be listed as follows:

(1) How the student will go about labeling the cultural contents of his study area depends largely on the quality and the abundance of available data and the scale and purpose of his study. There is no standard formula for recognizing a culture and drawing its boundaries, although some traits, such as language and economic structure, are much more serviceable than others. A distinctive combination of traits will determine the peculiar cultural personality of every area; but these traits can be recognized only after preliminary investigation.

(2) The past or present nature, and changes in the general cultural configuration of the area should be noted and their demographic effects appraised. Only rarely, and then generally for past eras, will apparent stability be discovered. Not only must shifts be reckoned with in current cause-and-effect relationships between culture and demography, but the lingering effects of past conditions must also be considered, for these may persist long after the initiating impulse has died away.

(3) Is the student confronted with a single culture that has only minor local variants, or is he dealing with two or more distinct entities? The research strategy for an area with a plural society, such as Trinidad, Malaya, or South Africa, or a highly diverse one, such as Hawaii or Israel, differs sharply from an area with the relative cultural monotony of Denmark, Newfoundland, or Eire.

(4) After the culture of an area has been identified, one should compare its population traits with those of ancestral cultures or with others that resemble the study area because of kinship or convergent evolution.

(5) The structure of each culture implies distinctive population characteristics. The immediate factors of demographic change are fertility, mortality, and migration, and a group's social structure, economic system, mating customs, diet, shelter, clothing, and medical practices all affect the pattern of births and deaths. Although some migrations are unique events engendered by unique circumstances, basic propensities in each culture influence the normal course of migration, or the lack of it. It is also usual to have some "feedback" from persistent population change, so that such change can modify the basic character of the culture. Such interrelations do, admittedly, comprise a rather obscure, but important, subject that needs to be clarified by further research.

(6) Each culture is closely associated with a particular economic pattern. One cannot be understood without the other, and each reacts powerfully upon the other. The great importance of the economic factor in shaping a society or culture (and thus its population patterns) is all too obvious. Yet it is only by understanding the full cultural context of a group that one can grasp, along with its identity and narrow functional aspects, such issues as what is or is not regarded as an economic resource; what is the intelligent way to use land, forest, and other resources; which occupations are honorific and which are odious; what is socially acceptable business practice—all these are implicit in the broad cultural

pattern.[6] Equally important in this world of rapid change and intensive communications, this larger pattern suggests how receptive the group will be to economic innovation or even revolution.

(7) The capacity of a people to absorb external influences—noneconomic as well as economic—and to interact with other peoples is one of the important facts to be gained from exploring the connotations of a given culture.

(8) Although many demographic correlates of a given culture cannot be specified now because we lack observation and analysis, even a futile search serves a useful purpose. The investigator is sensitized to the basic role of the cultural factor, and he will avoid an automatic ethnocentrism that ascribes the demographic assumptions of his own society to other groups.

If each culture has a distinctive personality, it would seem impossible to pigeonhole cultures into any system of universal categories. At best they can be sorted into genetically related families or into hierarchies of spatially or historically proximate areas. But in examining the cultural fact most important from the demographic point of view—the economic system and those phases of social organization closely dependent on mode of livelihood—several types or stages of socioeconomic development can be recognized in widely scattered parts of the world. The cultures that share membership in any given socioeconomic category will also share many population characteristics, even though each group will have other traits that are independent of its general socioeconomic structure. Thus each socioeconomic stage is an intercultural phenomenon shared by many groups of diverse noneconomic character. Conversely, within any culture area of appreciable size, more than one stage of socioeconomic development is likely to exist. Since it can be argued that these categories form a sequential, evolutionary series, one can approach them historically in a manner modified from the scheme developed by Hans Bobek.[7]

---

[6] There are not only such obvious examples as the negligible importance of vineyards in Islamic Southwest Asia, the absence of a beef-cattle culture in India, or the disdain with which farming is regarded by the cattle-obsessed élite of East Africa, but also such an apparently hard-headed phenomenon as commercial farming in the United States. The nature of this agricultural economy is mostly an arbitrary affair based on cultural postulates as to the relative value of land and money, familial values vs. commercial ones, and the relative prestige of various social and occupational roles. One need only look for comparisons with the French Canadian agricultural economy to see how largely both are derived from different, essentially arbitrary, cultural premises.

[7] "The Main Stages in Socioeconomic Evolution from a Geographic Point of View," in Philip L. Wagner and Marvin W. Mikesell, eds., *Readings in Cultural Geography,* pp. 218-47. Although the general evolutionary sequence postulated by Bobek seems indisputable, few scholars would contend that every community has gone through the specified series of stages in precisely the order and manner indicated. In particular, the diffusion of relatively advanced forms of socioeconomic organization from centers of innovation to less advanced areas can bring about sudden change, often several steps at a time. The most important series of such exports of an advanced type of human society, the "Europeanization of the World," is discussed on pp. 72-77.

CHAPTER NINE

The socioeconomic
evolution of mankind

Stages of Socioeconomic Development:
The Primitive Food-gathering Stage

When and where Homo sapiens emerged from an ancestral anthropoid stock may never be determined with certitude, but the best current opinion is that various human species appeared in East-Central Africa at least one million years ago.[1] It is, however, certain that this clever, unspecialized, and hence, highly adaptable biped wandered over a large part of the habitable Old World at an early date many tens, or even hundreds, of thousands of years ago, and then crossed over into the Americas via some Arctic route. Thousands of years elapsed between significant technological inventions, and during this time, man could be considered as little more than another large mammal, eating whatever game he could capture with his primitive weapons, and foraging for all the edible vegetable matter within reach. His impact upon the wild landscape was rather negligible, aside from such damage as was caused by man-made fires and the genetic effects of selective harvesting on plants and animals. Early man apparently was so dependent upon nature's generosity and so susceptible to environmental hazard that the study of his population geography would have been well within the province of the zoogeographer.

Almost no direct knowledge of the population characteristics of groups

[1] Among the more authoritative recent works on the origins of man are William W. Howells, *Mankind in the Making* (Garden City: Doubleday, 1959); L. S. B. Leakey, *The Progress and Evolution of Man in Africa* (New York: Oxford Univ., 1961); Carleton S. Coon, *The Story of Man* (New York: Knopf, 1962), and *The Origin of Races* (New York: Knopf, 1962).

in this primitive food-gathering stage exists because archaeology furnishes imperfect sample data and the various groups that survived into modern times and were analyzed by anthropologists had already been influenced by more advanced peoples.[2] It seems likely that both total numbers and gross population density were extremely low, for, outside a few well-endowed areas, it must have taken several square kilometers to sustain a single individual. Society consisted of isolated families or small bands of families, and the largest association was probably the extended kinship group, or clan. Only slight differentials in economic achievement were found among various geographic areas. Some sedentary populations may have developed where available resources were particularly abundant, but human existence was mainly nomadic and limited to those tracts where both food and potable water were normally at hand.[3] The few artifacts were made of stone, hides, bone, shell, wood, and other plant materials. A high mortality rate can be deduced from the general conditions of life. Life expectancy at birth was probably less than twenty years; disease and death, attributable largely to infectious or parasitic agents, violent accident, and occasionally, malnutrition, were prevalent. Warfare was probably at worst a minor, sporadic affair for lack of much economic surplus. A high birth rate can be postulated as a necessary strategy for group survival, but nothing useful can be said about sex ratios or about the racial, linguistic, and religious differences that undoubtedly existed. It is possible that cultural diversity was somewhat greater than economic diversity and that the demography of each group was distinctive within narrow limits.

At the beginning of the modern period, around A.D. 1500, the range of such primitive food collectors was already limited (see Map 4). Since the disappearance of such folk from the Great Basin section of the United States, northern Mexico, eastern Brazil, and southern South America, this primordial economy has been represented only by a few bands of Bushmen in South Africa, some Australian aborigines in the least desirable sections of that country, and small, partially acculturated groups of pygmoid stock in the least accessible recesses of the Congo Basin, montane Southeast Asia, and Malaysia. These paleolithic men are of very slight numerical or economic importance and may well lose the little that is left of their identity in the next few decades; but their theoretical significance to the social scientist remains great. As with all other groups of relatively lowly status, enough diffusion or imposition of cultural traits has been brought about by advanced urban-industrial peoples so that the present-day economy is somewhat hybridized.

[2] The economic life of hunting-and-gathering folk and other relatively primitive groups is treated in C. Daryll Forde, *Habitat, Economy and Society: A Geographical Introduction to Ethnology* (New York: Dutton, 1934) and Kaj Birket-Smith, *Primitive Man and His Ways* (London: Odhams, 1960).

[3] But this is not necessarily so. The Australian aborigines wandered everywhere within their continental range despite the abundant wild resources of some localities. In much of the rest of the world, the archaeological record for this earliest economic stage of mankind is too obscure for generalizations.

Specialized Collectors, Hunters, and Fishermen

The Upper Paleolithic and Mesolithic phases of human evolution saw an appreciable growth in man's inventiveness, and several more advanced modes of food collection appeared. In this stage of specialized collectors, hunters, and fishermen, various groups, possibly quite independently of one another, invented the technical implements necessary to exploit, and to live comfortably within, special ecological niches. More effective weapons and hunting strategies made possible the pursuit of large game, and often a single species was preferred on which not only the food supply, but the whole material culture as well, was predicated, i.e., shelter, fuel, clothing, weapons, household implements, toys, art objects, and vehicles, if any. Examples of this are the Eskimo seal complex, the caribou culture of the neighboring Amerindians, the importance of the American bison to the life of the Plains Indians, and the place of the moa in the economy of the Ur-Polynesians of New Zealand's South Island. Elsewhere, a firm material basis for society was provided by the abundance of certain plant foods: the acorns of central California, or the fish, shellfish, and other foodstuffs in favored shore zones, such as those in the Pacific Northwest, Florida and Georgia, or the littorals of Southeast Asia.

Assured of relative material abundance, these hunters, fishermen, and collectors were able to build larger, more complex societies than those built by their unspecialized forebears. Where the food supply was stationary, as in sections of coastal California or British Columbia, dense village settlement was feasible. A decided sexual division of labor appeared, along with the accentuation of the importance of age, and growing social and occupational complexity brought about the beginnings of social stratification. The hunting ethos and an economic surplus converted warfare into a popular institution. Again, we can only speculate about the demographic details of such populations; but the reproductive pattern must have been one of high fertility in order to balance an erratic but generally high rate of mortality. A low life expectancy meant a relatively large number of young, a distinct deficit of adults, and very few aged people.

Cultural advances in the Mesolithic period occasioned great areal diversity in population characteristics. Because of his generally expanded technology and larger capacity for mischief, man began to have a much greater effect upon the wild biota. In some areas, such as New Zealand's South Island or postglacial North America, many of the larger animals were hunted to extinction and the flora was impoverished by burning or other depredations. The great percentage of inhabited earth over which these specialized collectors, hunters, and fishermen must have ranged at one time was severely reduced by the arrival of farmers and nomadic pastoralists. Within modern times, the last significant groups of these specialized predators and collectors have been pushed into the Arctic and sub-Arctic portions of North America and Eurasia, and their culture has been greatly diluted by that of their more advanced neighbors.

Clan Peasantry

The exact time and place of what has probably been the most important advance in human history—the development of agriculture—may never be ascertained; but at least two independent centers can be postulated: southern Asia and tropical America.[4] The discovery of techniques for cultivating plants, at least 10,000 to 15,000 years ago in the Old World, possibly half as long ago in the Americas, meant that men were finally able to manufacture their food supplies and grow many of the raw materials that would be fabricated into clothing, shelter, tools, and a growing list of other products. This was the first decisive step toward control of the environment. The parallel and subsequent domestication of a variety of animals in both agricultural centers further enriched the subsistence base and helped to accelerate technological growth.

Initially, modes of cultivation were rudimentary, and socioeconomic development was hardly more advanced than it had been in the favored localities among specialized collectors, hunters, and fishermen. The basic communities were no larger than the village or the extended kinship group—sedentary where physical circumstances warranted, but mostly seminomadic in nature. But the superiority of the new economic system rapidly asserted itself, and the techniques of clan peasantry (following Bobek's terminology) spread at an early date to those portions of the Old World—Australia and South Africa excepted—where agriculture encountered no serious physical obstacles. In the New World, the agricultural revolution spread to the latitudinal limits of maize cultivation (southern Manitoba and central Chile), but failed somehow to reach such likely areas as the Pacific littoral of the United States and Canada and large portions of Brazil and Argentina. Increasing abundance and diversity of material goods marked the beginnings of functional divisions within communities; the contrasting economic roles of the sexes were more sharply defined, and the rudiments of regular trade appeared. Appreciable advances in nutrition must surely have brought about a slow but substantial increase in human numbers—the first faltering step toward death control.

Man's occupance of the earth's surface was now both more intensive and extensive than during his long ecological apprenticeship. Forests and marshes were replaced by fields, and farmers erupted into grassland areas, profoundly disturbing flora and fauna. The soil itself underwent major modifications, and in some instances the very contours of the land

---

[4] The origins of agriculture are treated in Carl O. Sauer, *Agricultural Origins and Dispersals* (New York: American Geographical Soc., 1952) and E. C. Curwen and Gudmund Hatt, *Plough and Pasture: The Early History of Farming* (New York: Schuman, 1953).

were reshaped. Although wide gaps still existed between occupied tracts because of various military or political reasons, or because of obscure cultural factors, a sizeable fraction of the habitable earth was being "humanized." In a few instances, a hybrid economy emerged combining the predatory-collecting and the agrarian systems. This was conspicuously so in the eastern two-thirds of the United States where the aborigines never fully discarded the chase for the hoe.

The discussion of clan peasantries involves much more than historic reconstruction. With its special economic, psychological, and demographic traits, clan peasantry has persisted with remarkable tenacity even within regions where revolutionary social and economic forms have been added to the older ones at a rapid rate. Many isolated relics of the clan-peasantry system can be found in rural sections of Western Europe alongside immeasurably more sophisticated areas; it is even possible to detect the transference of certain clan-peasantry traits from Europe to the New World. Clan peasantries linger on or are even dominant in the less advanced, remoter portions of southern Asia, the southwest Pacific, Africa, and aboriginal America. It is interesting to note that as the socioeconomic scale is ascended and development and dispersal of new systems becomes more rapid, the supplanting of old forms by the new seems less thoroughgoing.

Shortly after the introduction of farming in the Old World, nomadic pastoralism appeared, probably within the same seminal Southwest Asian region that is most likely one of the original homes of agriculture. Subsisting on the flesh and milk of goats, sheep, cattle, and somewhat later, horses, asses, camels, and reindeer—in fact, basing almost their entire material existence on the carcasses of their flocks—these herdsmen were able to penetrate and effectively exploit, at least seasonally, the extensive tracts too waterless, cool, or rough for successful farming. This appears to have happened in the steppes and deserts of southern Russia and Central Asia and the tundra of northern Eurasia. In other instances the mobile, warlike nomad was able to wrest perfectly adequate cropland from the farmer or reduce him to servile status. We see, then, that various forms of symbiosis embrace nomad and peasant in North Africa, the Sudan, much of East Africa, and many parts of Southwest Asia. This may well be the only instance where a later socioeconomic system (if, in fact, it is more recent) represents a lower over-all population density than an antecedent one. The settlement forms—and probably also the demography—of the nomadic groups are distinctive, the relationships of man, space, and resources being unlike anything else encountered by the population geographer.

A sudden flowering of the hidden resources of the human mind and society was touched off by the agricultural revolution. The irrevocable plunge into a complex, uncertain, but richer future had begun. Each new tool, technique, or scientific fact was followed by another. After clan peasantry had been widely adopted, either voluntary or forced confederations of local groups began to spring up in many areas, probably first in Southwest Asia, but then in many other parts of the Old World and in Middle America and the Andean country as well. The danger of nomadic raids may have catalyzed the process in Mesopotamia, Iran, the Levant, and Egypt, but the internal logic of material abundance could well have been the critical factor. Political units based on military force rather than on kinship ties were extensive, though often poorly organized. Their emergence meant larger villages and even embryonic cities; the agricultural colonization of much interstitial land that had previously been idle; the beginnings of areal specialization in production, and thus regular commerce; and a definite stratification of society that provided for an administrative, military, and often priestly élite.

Advanced Rural and Urban Civilizations

At this point several major themes appear that become more pertinent as higher systems are encountered. Basic to the growing complexity of society and economy is a relaxation of the direct bonds between man and earth (or more precisely, between a given group and a given parcel of land) and between the individual and his kinship or neighborhood group. Instead, men became more dependent on distant communities for goods, services, ideas, and ultimately, recreation; interregional relationships multiply at a geometric rate. The human family increases in numbers, but as the crosscurrent of individuals, objects, and messages quickens, one can discern the outlines of a single universal community, however imperfect it may be.

A related theme states that advancing technology breeds rich local diversity—at least until this diversity is partially overtaken by the superficial standardization of form and ideas that seems to flow from the highly efficient communications of the present day. Beneath this apparent homogenization, however, the areal differentiation of areas and populations in terms of functions still proceeds apace. Less fortunately, the higher man is on the socioeconomic scale, the greater is his capacity to alter the face of the earth. Primitive society was able to chip away slowly at the soils and biota of its surroundings; advanced society is not only able to act much more intensively and rapidly on soils, plants, and animals, but it has even taken much mineral wealth from the crust of the earth, greatly reworking the surface configuration of that crust in many places. The waters on and near the surface of the earth, as well as the very atmosphere itself, have also been modified, usually for the worse.[5] It is not surprising to discover that as man has advanced, he has institutionalized his latent instincts for self-destruction. For the past several thousand years, organized warfare and conquest have been intrinsic

[5] The most comprehensive treatment of this vast subject is in William L. Thomas, Jr., ed., *Man's Role in Changing the Face of the Earth* (Chicago: Univ. of Chicago, 1956).

features of relatively advanced societies, with their ample supplies of material goods, leisure, and mobility; though waged intermittently, warfare has thus long been a population factor of appreciable, and sometimes critical, importance for all too many communities.

It is not feasible to trace in detail here the rise of the rural civilizations under princely or feudal domination that frequently appeared in both the Old and the New Worlds, under favorable social and physical conditions, after the clan peasantries. Many such groups still exist in portions of West Africa and Southeast Asia, but in other parts of the world, after a relatively brief period most of these princely or feudal confederations gave way to urban civilizations of the rent-capitalist type.[6] It appears that Southwest Asia led again in this development; the earliest urban states were set up in the zone bounded by the Indus and Nile valleys, perhaps some 6,000 years ago. Gradually, this new kind of socioeconomic organization spread northeastward into Central Asia, China, Korea, and Japan, and southeastward into most of India and Ceylon; it penetrated less deeply into parts of Indochina and the East Indies. In the West, Phoenician, Hellenic, and Roman enterprise initiated the urban way of life into all corners of the Mediterranean and later into Northwest Europe. Within the New World, urban cultures evolved only in central and southern Mexico, the Yucatan, the Mayan sections of Guatemala, Honduras, and El Salvador, and portions of the Andean highlands and nearby coast.

The advent of the city brought with it rapid intensification of all kinds of economic activity, and a much more potent, stable control of government than had ever before been known. In addition to this, technological advancement was greatly stimulated. We shall mention only the most momentous inventions: the appearance and elaboration of metal tools; writing (and thus the storage of human experience in durable form); organized education and the first faint glimmerings of formal scientific procedures; the development of complex vehicles and systematic transportation networks. Urban communities varied greatly in areal extent, from the minute city-state that had no more than the single *polis* and its immediate hinterland, to the unwieldy Persian, Roman, or Incan empires. The physical security and economic efficiency of the urban system made possible much larger, denser populations than had ever before been witnessed. Indeed, the rural densities of southern and eastern Asia have never been surpassed by any subsequent forms of social organization. Exploitation of the soil by traditional means became more intensive and the introduction of new crops, animals, tools, and methods

[6] Among the more important treatments of the origins of cities are Lewis Mumford, *The City in History: Its Origins, Its Transformations, and Its Prospects* (New York: Harcourt, 1961); Robert J. Braidwood, *Courses Toward Urban Life* (Chicago: Aldine, 1962); Gideon Sjoberg, *The Preindustrial City, Past and Present* (New York: Free Press of Glencoe, 1960), pp. 25-51; and R. M. Adams, "The Origin of Cities," *Scientific American*, Vol. 203, No. 3 (September 1960), 3-10.

from distant areas was greatly facilitated. Local deficiencies in food, minerals, lumber, and a variety of manufactured necessities could be made good through organized commerce, thereby encouraging the aggregation of larger communities.

Demographically speaking, these urban civilizations stood apart from preceding socioeconomic systems in that for the first time, populations could be classified in terms of residence, literacy, and education. Class stratification of society was much more sharply defined, and occupational groupings became more elaborate and more distinct. Alongside the numerically dominant tillers of the soil and other primary producers, many persons engaged in the secondary and tertiary industries: small-scale manufacturing, transport, the military, commerce (with its complement of merchants and their clerks), personal services, administration, and a corps of priest-scholars. Nutrition, housing, clothing, and medical care improved somewhat—at least for the more fortunate members of society, lowering mortality rates and increasing life expectancy. The mingling of peoples through trade, conquest, or spontaneous migration caused what had once been almost homogeneous communities to be succeeded by those in which racial, ethnic, linguistic, and religious diversity were commonplace.

In spite of all their advantages over older systems, the urban civilizations of the rent-capitalist type suffered from one serious flaw—their rent-capitalist structure. Nearly all available capital was invested in land and agricultural labor; only the necessary minimum was given to commerce, transportation, or manufacturing. The result was virtually no growth in the capacities of the economy, at least after these civilizations had spread into hospitable territories and had achieved a comfortable equilibrium. And so, after a burst of creativity, these communities tended to stagnate for centuries or even millennia (Southwest Asia and India are cases in point). Some such societies have even retrogressed or decayed completely, although it is unfair to attribute their misfortune entirely to intrinsic socioeconomic weaknesses; here North African, Mayan, coastal Peruvian, Cambodian, and Mesopotamian examples come to mind. But whatever their shortcomings, these communities, though greatly modified today, still account for a larger percentage of the world's inhabitants than are found within any other socioeconomic stage.

Occidental Urban Civilization

All the systems examined so far have evolved rather leisurely and have attained some kind of dynamic equilibrium with their terrestrial and social environments. Occidental urban civilization, the most recent and formidable socioeconomic system, developed differently. The emergence of this most technologically advanced system in Northwest Europe within the past 500 years is a mysterious, awe-inspiring event for which there is as yet no plausible explanation. The seminal area—France, the Low Countries, the Rhineland, England, and northern Italy—had all, except for the Italian city-states, been areas of no great consequence during antiquity; moreover, they lacked any outstanding physical resources. Yet this region did, somehow, absorb and retain the lessons of Roman civilization, and it managed to continue to enrich its agricultural and industrial technology during the so-called "Dark Ages." By the thirteenth century, certain developments can be detected: the gradual revivification of urban life and commerce, new industrial processes, certain innovations in banking, and an incipient intellectual and aesthetic ferment quite unlike anything of the past. By the fifteenth century, modern "productive capitalism," with its propulsive blend of acquisitiveness, curiosity, and aggressiveness, had clearly emerged in Flanders and a few other advanced localities, and the first probes into the non-European world were being taken gingerly by explorer-merchants from Atlantic and Mediterranean ports. To an increasing degree, money was being invested in commerce and manufacturing rather than being put back into agrarian enterprise.

After the discovery of the New World and circum-African routes to the Orient, the progress of Western Europe's commerce and industry and its general social, cultural, and demographic development continued at an accelerating rate.[7] To borrow a familiar analogy from chemistry and physics, the mass and concentration of certain technological and psychological elements somehow reached that critical point at which a self-breeding, accelerating reaction set in. The most far-reaching effect of the relatively abrupt rise of productive capitalism has been the replacement of slow-change or near-stability regimes by a highly unstable system that is breeding material wealth, new scientific and technological ideas, new cultural values, and fresh forms of social organization ever more rapidly. It has created a universal expectation of a better way of life, even among those peoples as yet only slightly influenced by "European" ways. The geographic implications of this system are so immense that they obliterate, in the minds of many, the social and economic patterns engendered by earlier, less dynamic systems; however, the latter are still present and very much a part of contemporary reality.

The Western European brand of productive capitalism was taken to many parts of the world by the emigration and business activities of Europeans and by the general diffusion of its central ideas. The latter process—and the appearance of the proper economic preconditions—accounts for the "development" during the nineteenth and twentieth centuries of the remainder of Germany, of Scandinavia, portions of southern Europe, Russia, Eastern Europe and the Balkans, and Japan. It matters little in fundamental socioeconomic terms, though vastly in the

---

[7] There is no single comprehensive work covering the socioeconomic and technological ascendancy of Western Europe, but the theme is strongly developed in many general histories, for example, William H. McNeill, *The Rise of the West: A History of the Human Community* (Chicago: Univ. of Chicago, 1963). Two major treatises on the rise of capitalism: Henri See, *Modern Capitalism: Its Origin and Evolution* (New York: Adelphi, 1928) and Robert L. Heilbroner, *The Making of Economic Society* (Englewood Cliffs: Prentice-Hall, 1962).

political realm, whether the systems in question are labeled "free enter-prise" or "socialism." Their familial resemblances are more fundamental than the intrafamily differences. Many other areas, such as India, China, Mexico, or North Korea, have attempted to emulate the West-ern European model; there have been no decisive results as yet. The massive outpouring of Europeans ensured the successful grafting of the new capitalism onto Anglo-America, middle-latitude South America, South Africa, Australia, New Zealand, Siberia, and smaller corners elsewhere.

Almost the entire non-European world was brought under the eco-nomic suzerainty of Europe, and where direct political control could be discreetly imposed, this, too, was done. Not only was the flow of raw materials, manufactured goods, and various services involved; the process also encompassed the export of languages and religions, political, philosophical, and other cultural cargo, and ways of life in general. It was a massive, pervasive thrust of European folk and practices, and its greatest effect was to stimulate the rest of the world to equal aspira-tion. The intense, often destructive, exploitation of much of the soil, mineral, woodland, animal, and marine wealth of the "colonial" areas was another major result of the European expansion. This despoilment seriously complicated the subsequent task of providing the local popula-tion with the kind of existence they had just been taught to desire.

The European Demographic Revolution

While Western Europe was fixing its imprint upon the entire planet, startling demographic developments were taking place at home, the ultimate effects of which may well be as serious for the overseas terri-tories as the initial economic and political impact had been.[8] The upsurge in Western Europe's economy was accompanied by major incre-ments in the size and complexity of its population. Rural densities appeared to grow only slightly; indeed, at a later stage, pronounced rural depopulation became a widespread phenomenon among European societies as mass moves to cities and foreign lands continued. Instead, population growth centered in cities; in terms of size, number, complexity of function, and nearness to each other, they far outclassed all earlier forms of urban development. (Such situations encourage a growing community of interests between population and urban geographers.) Employment in the primary industries lagged far behind the rapid growth of the manufacturing labor force and the transport, wholesale, and retail trade, other "tertiary" occupations, and later, the "quaternary" industries, i.e., the professional and skilled service occupations. In gen-

---

[8] Basic materials, and thus, scholarly analyses, on the Western European demo-graphic revolution have been abundant for Great Britain. For a summary discussion of the topic in a British context—and references to the more important literature—see William Petersen, *Population* (New York: Macmillan, 1961), pp. 376-404.

eral, giant strides were made in the fields of literacy and education. Considerable fluidity in personal income and class status began to develop, and one of the more significant symptoms of the individualism basic to early productive capitalism was the unprecedented degree of atomistic spatial mobility. The great flood of migrants to the "new lands" was mainly a movement of single families and individuals rather than the tribe or nation of the older traditional pattern. That unique combination of empty lands, self-financed migrants, and a world hungry for the fruits of their labor occupied an instant in world history that could never again be duplicated.

The development of "death control" was a most significant product of the vast scientific revolution accompanying the industrial revolution, the agricultural revolution, and other such spurts in technology. Owing to better nutrition, public hygiene, elementary improvements in child care, more advanced systems of communication and transportation, the beginnings of a modern hospital system, a higher valuation of human life, and the discovery of means to control many forms of infectious disease, death rates underwent a major decline sometime during the eighteenth century. After a delay of several decades (for reasons still not fully explained), birth rates also began to decline, and in a few instances during the 1930's, they actually dipped below death rates. (See columns 12 and 17 in the Appendix.) Because of the delayed onset of low-fertility patterns and the persistence for some time thereafter of a wide gap between births and deaths, the population of Europe enjoyed a remarkably large, rapid growth despite massive emigration and many sporadic wars. European populations now have an age structure, fertility pattern, and age-specific mortality schedule that is quite distinctive, namely, a relatively mature population with low birth rates and even lower death rates—a humane regime that efficiently replenishes its numbers.[9]

One of the colossal ironies of human history has been the way in which European methods of death control have been effectively exported in recent years. Many regions have as yet hardly begun significant economic development, and thus, unlike Europe, they are ill-equipped for the great additions to labor force and numbers of dependents that follow the rapid decline in mortality rates. Close contacts between European and neo-European lands on the one hand, and the so-called underdeveloped lands on the other, are necessary for their mutual survival; yet such contacts have led to dangerous runaway population growth in the latter because the European pattern of family limitation has not proved so readily exportable. The consideration of a discordant death rate and many other items as well make it clear that however

[9] Compare the "European" countries in the Appendix (those listed in the "Highly Advanced" and "Advanced" sections) with the "Transitional" and "Underdeveloped" countries in terms of demographic indices, specifically items 5-21. Because the 41 countries in this Appendix are listed in order of approximate socioeconomic level, the table lends itself to a number of comparisons—social and economic, as well as demographic.

vital the classification of socioeconomic development may be for the population geographer, such simple identification is not sufficient. He must also understand how much grafting of different systems has occurred—where, how, and at what rate.

Partial Europeanization
of the Non-European World

The full graphic representation of the Europeanization of the world lies beyond the resources of even the craftiest cartographer, even assuming that enough raw data exists, but Maps 5 and 6 offer a rough draft of a bewildering situation. Map 5 depicts the degree of demographic and political penetration made by Europeans, Map 6, the degree of economic development along Western European lines. There is, of course, a marked degree of covariance between the two drawings.

The creation of the neo-European tracts shown in Map 5, by a process of migration to regions that are endowed with either an inviting set of untouched natural resources or physical surroundings not too dissimilar from those of the homeland, was necessarily limited to a small fraction of the previously non-European world. A small, highly vigorous corps of migrants carried political and economic influences from Europe to a much broader territory. In cases such as most of Siberia, Kazakhstan, New Zealand's North Island, Israel, and Alaska, the newcomers were either unable or unwilling to eradicate the indigenous inhabitants, and they have managed to live side by side with them in the permanent roles of colonist and benevolent overlord. In many other cases, such as South Africa, the Rhodesias, Angola, Kenya, and the Caucasus, the resident European minority has maintained the upper hand politically and economically, even though the permanence of the arrangement may be somewhat questionable. In such instances as the former Japanese colonial empire, where the Japanese played the part of surrogate Europeans, or in Algeria, Mexico, and to a variable extent, in other parts of former New Spain, the power of the ruling minority of invaders has been largely or fully broken.

An even more extensive part of the non-European world must be classed as politically, but not demographically, colonial. Here a small band of European soldiers, administrators, businessmen, technicians, and missionaries contrived to exercise dominion over large territories on behalf of the metropolitan governments without themselves becoming a part of the locality. Where European control was prolonged and effective (in some cases it persisted for more than three centuries), the impact on culture, economy, and demography has been far-reaching. Where control was transient or shallow, the effects have been correspondingly weaker, though they have been far from trivial. Even where independence from European rule has been nominally maintained, as in Liberia, Afghanistan, or Thailand, Europeanization has progressed appreciably.

Plantation Societies

Plantation society is a peculiar category that falls outside the continuum just sketched. It came into being wherever there were obvious possibilities for enrichment through large-scale corporate agricultural or mineral enterprise in the colonial world under a capitalistic system. Where an adequate supply of volunteer indigenous or European labor was not available, it was necessary to import large numbers of alien slaves or indentured workers, or to alter radically pre-existing systems of land tenure, as happened in parts of Latin America and Africa. The system was developed experimentally with some success in the Canary and Cape Verde Islands (and later, further south in African waters in Saõ Tomé, Principé, and Fernando Poo); it was exported to the Caribbean, Brazil, and the warmer parts of British North America at the first opportunity. Despite much local variation in detail, telltale signs in the demography and social structure of the Antilles, the Guianas, the Caribbean coast of Central America, the southeastern United States, and much of the Brazilian littoral reveal that the plantation system was once, or still is, dominant. The violent, or at best, unpleasant genesis of these new societies was softened in the American South and Brazil by the fact that in those two areas, unlike the usual Caribbean situation, owners were not absentees or transient entrepreneurs; they were local residents. Also, these were composite societies with large numbers of free persons residing alongside the slave groups.

The mixture of Negroid and Asian elements found in Trinidad and the Guianas makes these areas closely akin to Mauritius, Réunion, Fiji, and a few other Indian and Pacific isles that must also be classified as plantation areas. The plantation society of Malaya, like that of Natal, is sui generis in its combination of ethnic elements. Though not so overt as to be recognized as such on the map, strong internal plantation tendencies can also be detected within such countries as the former Belgian Congo, South Africa, Indonesia, Ceylon, and India, where there has been a massive flow of labor—perhaps not without some subtle coercion—from well-populated regions to those deficient in workers but rich in economic promise.

The differential levels of economic development shown in Map 6 (and the demographic concomitants not shown) are the outcome of the complex interplay of many forces. Among these forces are: the volume of the flow of European migrants and capital; the strength and longevity of foreign control; the richness and exploitability of local resources; and the initiative of the local populace. The differential levels do not merely represent the diffusion of Europeans and their ways. Japan's upward economic leap and the incipient development of China, Hong Kong, Taiwan, India, North Korea, Kuwait, Puerto Rico, Mexico, and Cuba are the results of local energies catalyzed by European example. Also note that the extensive areas classed as "isolated tribal economies" are not

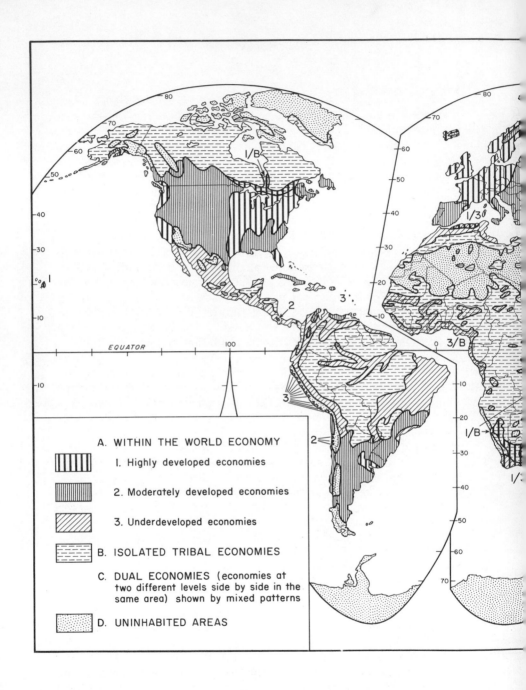

A. WITHIN THE WORLD ECONOMY

|||||| 1. Highly developed economies

|||||| 2. Moderately developed economies

////// 3. Underdeveloped economies

====== B. ISOLATED TRIBAL ECONOMIES

C. DUAL ECONOMIES (economies at two different levels side by side in the same area) shown by mixed patterns

······ D. UNINHABITED AREAS

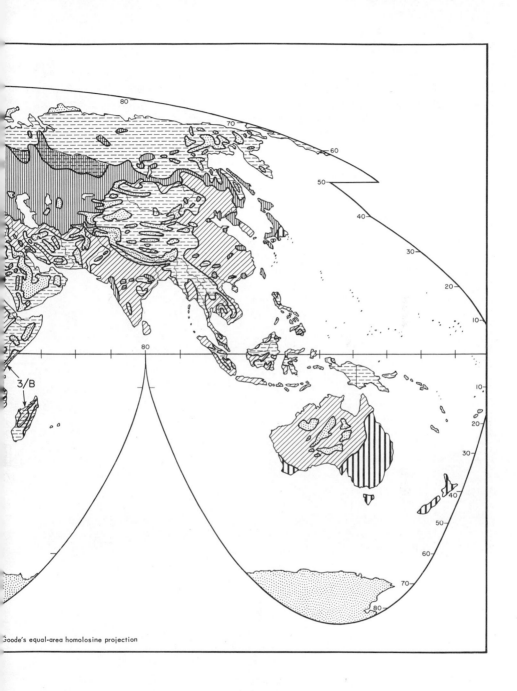

3/B

Goode's equal-area homolosine projection

6. Levels of Economic Development (ca. 1955)

quite as isolated or untouched as might appear from a necessarily over-simplified map. Almost without exception, the residents of such areas participate in world commerce, at least in a marginal way, and have, in turn, had their societies and economic systems partially transformed in recent years.

CHAPTER TEN

Population regions
and the larger world

The External Relations
of Population Regions

The external relations of a region make up the third basic element in this typology of population regions. Besides being implicit in basic cultural patterns and stage of socioeconomic development, it is quite important in its own right. The proposition that the size, structure, functions, and areal dimensions of any given population are strongly conditioned by its dealings with other parts of the world is too self-evident to call for any elaborate defense. Only a society of the most primitive level is the genesis of the population pattern confined to the interaction of a group and its culture with the local environment.

External relations are too specific to classify each region areally or historically. Perhaps the most fruitful approach would be to analyze the source or destination, volume, and significance of the three distinct strands that link an area to the rest of the world: movement of people, movement of goods and services, and movement of ideas. Such an approach might well be expressed in terms of dominance or dependence. In some instances, a given area will initiate migration, economic transactions, and ideas; in others, it is the recipient, and in still other instances, some elements are transmitted and some are absorbed. But because there is so little duplication of past or present situations, it is doubtful whether a satisfactory simple typology of external relations can ever be devised. A few examples will illustrate the importance and complexity of this factor.

New Zealand, Brazil, and Germany

New Zealand's external relations are uncomplicated compared to those of other regions, and since its settlement by Europeans during the nineteenth century, it has been strongly dependent on its relationship with a single European power—Great Britain.[1] Virtually all New Zealanders, except the native Maori, are of British immigrant stock. Great Britain has been the principal, and dominant, trading partner, and has donated nearly all the political, educational, literary, intellectual, and other cultural elements prevalent in New Zealand. Recent acceleration in the nation's industrialization and closer commercial ties with the United States and Australia have made the pattern of external ties less simple; but it is hardly likely that, given New Zealand's remoteness and small population, it will become a major transmitter of people, ideas, industrial goods, or political power. The population student will probably not be able to ignore the vital connection with Great Britain for some time to come.

Nations such as Brazil represent the other extreme.[2] There the basic ingredients of an unusually varied population are drawn from many sources: Portugal, the original colonizing power, and later, other portions of southern Europe; from many distinct African tribes, as well as from that larger Negro group not assignable to specified sections of Africa; from Germany and other parts of Central and Eastern Europe; from Japan; and from many diverse aboriginal groups. Although Brazil has continued to admit immigrants in significant numbers, most of these newcomers soon become identified with the general Brazilian population, and unlike the New Zealanders, generally lose a sense of identification with the source area. During Brazil's colonial period, its commerce was largely controlled by Portugal, but there were also large-scale dealings with the Netherlands, Germany, Great Britain, and other European maritime powers. More recently, the United States has become Brazil's dominant trading partner, though not to the exclusion of other nations. In terms of culture and ideas, Brazil has been notably eclectic. Although Portugal was the prime contributor for a long time, each of the other large groups of immigrants has added its quota to the melting pot of Brazilian culture. Brazil has turned to France, and more recently,

---

[1] For a good general introduction to New Zealand's geography, including a discussion of overseas transport and trade, consult Kenneth B. Cumberland, *Southwest Pacific: A Geography of Australia, New Zealand, and their Pacific Island Neighborhood* (London: Methuen, 1956), pp. 175-249. New Zealand's demography is treated in detail in New Zealand, Ministry of Works, Town and Country Planning Board, *A Survey of New Zealand Population* (Wellington, 1960). Some of the information on New Zealand in the Appendix is relevant to this discussion.

[2] An excellent introduction to Brazilian demography and society is provided in T. Lynn Smith, *Brazil: People and Institutions* (Baton Rouge: Louisiana State Univ., 1954). The nature and origins of Brazilian culture are analyzed brilliantly in Gilberto Freyre, *The Masters and the Slaves: A Study in the Development of Brazilian Civilization* (New York: Knopf, 1946).

to the United States for the advanced elements in its intellectual life. As a recipient of settlers, ideas, and industrial goods, this nation has been decidedly colonial for the past four centuries. However, signs of the attainment of a more equal status with other nations are visible. Its growing strength and maturity has enabled Brazil to export some of its own literature, dances, and music to the rest of the world and to achieve some degree of autonomy in certain branches of science.

Germany's position is very different from that of either New Zealand or Brazil.[3] During Roman and early medieval times, the Germanic tribes, and later states, were largely passive recipients of external influences; in recent centuries, Germany has risen to a station of general dominance in its traffic with the non-German world. Thickly populated colonies of Germans lodged in numerous localities throughout Eastern Europe from the thirteenth century onward, and a sense of community with the homeland was preserved, with important consequences for Germany and the other nations, at least until the great ingathering of the Volksdeutsch in the 1940's. A short-lived colonial empire was of little significance for the homeland, but the Germans have emigrated enthusiastically to many overseas destinations. More conscientious than most other European immigrant groups in clinging to some lasting identification with the mother country, their efforts have not been entirely successful. Recently, the exodus of Germans has dwindled considerably, largely because of a need for the manpower that a flourishing economy requires. The number of people leaving is balanced by the inflow of labor migrants from other parts of Europe. Germany has held its dominant position in the trade of Central Europe and many non-European countries despite its recent split into two political entities; and its symbiotic commercial relations with many partners is an essential element in the understanding of its demography. Germany has also exercised widespread influence as one of the leading exporters of science and technology, besides making many important contributions to the field of fine arts.

Greece, California, Sweden, and Others

The element of change is as implicit in external relations as it is in other components of this typology. A few examples will show how variable the nature of a region's external dealings can be. Early in their history, the Greek city-states gained commercial control of much of the Mediterranean Basin and set up numerous colonies along its shores. Ultimately, the Macedonians attained political mastery over most of the known civilized world, though they held their power only briefly. Greece was also the fountainhead of an extraordinary wealth of political, philosophical, scientific, and technological notions. But after this early efflores-

---

[3] The literature on Germany is extensive. Among the relatively accessible books relevant to this discussion are Robert E. Dickinson, *Germany: A General and Regional Geography* (New York: Dutton, 1953) and Jethro Bethell, *Germany: A Companion to German Studies*, 5th ed. (London: Methuen, 1955).

cence, Greece became politically subordinate to Rome and its successor states, and later to the Ottoman Empire, before it regained a precarious independence in the early nineteenth century. Its sovereignty has been subject to the veto of whatever greater power looms over the eastern Mediterranean at the moment, whether it be Great Britain, Germany, or the United States. Despite its political weakness, Greece continues to export people—but no longer under its own terms to places of its own choosing. In the realms of commerce and ideas, modern Greece remains the subordinate partner in almost any exchange.[4]

The trend has been just the opposite in California.[5] From a weak, sparsely settled, isolated area—the colony of a colony—subservient in terms of migration, commerce, and culture, California has risen to a much more enviable estate. It continues to import great numbers of people, but under conditions that benefit California more than the regions from which these people come. Although California is far from being economically autonomous, it is becoming increasingly less dependent on other regions for advanced services and industrial and consumer goods; indeed, it exports them to much of the western part of North America. California has become an influential center for culture. Its impact has been felt in such fields as architecture, fashion, the cinema, and various aspects of modern living. Anyone using an historical approach to the population geography of California would be obliged to refer constantly to these changing external linkages in order to make his analysis intelligible.

Finally, radical transformations in population geography is revealed by the shifting migratory patterns (and other external relations) of such lands as Sweden, Puerto Rico, and Jamaica. The major outpouring of Sweden's citizens to the United States and Canada during the past century enabled this nation to handle the problems brought on by deep economic and demographic change; it must now solicit significant numbers of Finnish workers for its highly developed economy. Jamaica was hindered by labor shortages for a long period; it had to import African workers on a large scale, and to a lesser degree, East Indians and Chinese. Spain encouraged both the slave trade and the entry of Spanish settlers to bolster the Puerto Rican economy. Today the demography of the two islands has been greatly altered; both now export large numbers of surplus inhabitants in order to function effectively (Jamaica to Great Britain and certain sparsely settled parts of the Caribbean; Puerto Rico to the United States).

[4] See Ellen Churchill Semple, The Geography of the Mediterranean Region: Its Relation to Ancient History (New York, 1911); Y. Chataigneau and J. Sion, "La Grèce," Géographie Universelle, VII, Part A (Paris: Colin, 1934), 512-75; and Wilbert E. Moore, Economic Demography of Eastern and Southern Europe (Geneva: League of Nations, 1945).

[5] The historical geography of California is treated in Ralph H. Brown, Historical Geography of the United States (New York: Harcourt, 1948), pp. 76-81, 501-32, and William L. Thomas, Jr., ed., "Man, Time, and Space in Southern California: A Symposium," Annals of the Association of American Geographers, Vol. 49, No. 3, Part 2 (September 1959).

The factor of external relations is as highly relevant for small areas as it is for whole continents. Indeed it becomes increasingly critical in approaching the populations of smaller communities where ties to the rest of the nation, as well as to foreign areas, are of paramount importance. The population of any locality, beyond the very simplest, cannot be understood except as a phenomenon in constant flux, involved in many complex relationships with factors that are at some remove as well as in the immediate vicinity. These long-distance interchanges of people, commodities, and ideas must be fully appreciated within their political contexts and be integrated into a taxonomy of population regions if the geographer is to understand such regions.

CHAPTER ELEVEN

The balance of
people and resources

The Population/Resource Ratio.
What is a Resource?

The fourth and final element in this typology of population regions
is the relationship between the size and technical adequacy of a population on the one hand and the quantity and quality of terrestrial resources
on the other, i.e., the population/resource ratio. The casual onlooker
might regard this as the most "geographic" element. Here at last, it would
seem, a classificatory system based on the innate cultural personality of
the community, its socioeconomic status, and its connections with external
communities, could be grounded in the phenomena of the physical
milieu. A closer look, however, suggests that even though the popula-
tion/resource ratio is intimately concerned with environmental facts (as
is also the case, though less overtly, with the other three factors in this
classification), the ratio is nonetheless basically man-oriented.

The highly variegated patterns of land occupance, the placement and
density of people, and the intensity with which they exploit their immediate surroundings are, to a significant degree, expressions of the
physical attributes of the locality and the resources available there. But
what determines whether a given substance or a physical attribute of a
place is to be considered and used as a resource?[1] The answer, except

[1] The resource concept is defined and its various ramifications explored in Walter
Firey, *Man, Mind and Land: A Theory of Resource Use* (New York: Free Press of
Glencoe, 1960); Harold J. Barnett and Chandler Morse, *Scarcity and Growth: The
Economics of Natural Resource Availability* (Baltimore: Johns Hopkins, 1963); and
Erich W. Zimmerman, *World Resources and Industries,* rev. ed. (New York: Harper,
1951). After its theoretical introduction, the Zimmerman volume concentrates on a
systematic analysis of specific resources and industries. Other important surveys of

for the most primitive hunting-and-gathering societies, is dictated less by the intrinsic nature of the potential resource than by the character or the broad resource capabilities of the people themselves.

A "resource" may be defined as any substance or physical property of a place that can in some way be used to satisfy a human need. Resources include the physical and biological potentialities of the minerals, soils, biota, water, and atmosphere of the locality—as they can be realized by its occupants—and whatever transportational, military, or recreational value may accrue through the interests and activities of local or distant peoples. In extremely primitive groups, where our approach is similar to that of the animal ecologist, the resource inventory may consist wholly of wild food and the immediately available rock, plant, and animal materials that can be easily converted into clothing, shelter, and tools. Among all other groups, a resource is the progeny of human aspiration, memory, talent, and labor applied to relatively inert physical entities. As human appetites grow and technologies become more advanced, so also may the available resources of a given place. Indeed we may never be able to assess the ultimate resource potential of any area beyond the certain fact that it is finite. We cannot determine the maximum attainable yield of corn in a given section of rich Illinois prairie or of rice per hectare in a Japanese field one hundred years from now. Neither can we tally the ultimate worth of a ton of coal or a cord of wood until all present and future chemical laboratories have been consulted. The ocean may well become the great purveyor of food and minerals for future populations, and it is conceivable that most of our needs for metals and energy can be satisfied by milling ordinary granite. Not even common clay should be overlooked.

Let us disregard the size of a community's population and territory for the moment. The adequacy of a community's resources depends mainly on its socioeconomic level, cultural attitudes, and hence, its capacity to exploit the physical properties of a given site and to arrange the circulation of commodites and personnel within and beyond its territory so as to gain the optimum advantage of its material circumstances. A low level of resources in a country may only reflect scarcity of financial and social capital and need not be a chronic condition. The introduction of ideas, technicians, and funds from outside will almost immediately raise the value of an area (as will a slow, autonomous evolution over the years). Cases in point are the impact of modern ground-water technologies on the Texas Panhandle, the sudden mineral ascendancy of the Kuznetsk Basin, and the transformation of Venezuela from a poor country to one of Latin America's most affluent regions, owing to the discovery and development of major petroleum and iron ore deposits by

resource availability and use include W. S. Woytinsky and E. S. Woytinsky, *World Population and Production: Trends and Outlook* (New York: Twentieth Century Fund, 1953); L. Dudley Stamp, *Our Undeveloped World* (London: Faber, 1953); and William Van Royen, *Atlas of the World's Resources* (Englewood Cliffs: Prentice-Hall, 1954).

foreign enterprise. The direct relevance of the physical environment to the population/resource ratio is further invalidated by the fact that, except among groups existing outside the market economy, the individual does not wrest his subsistence from his immediate surroundings. Instead, he must seek a supply of money, generally through employment, whereby physical and social wants can be satisfied by his purchasing goods and services that often originate at distant points.

The appraisal of each significant community resource is a matter of intense, abiding concern for the economic geographer, but the population geographer is taken up with the sufficiency of the *sum* of known, accessible resources, and the ratio (and by implication, the pressure) of population to these resources. This fourth element in the typology is unlike the other three in that it is meaningful only when applied either to a whole nation or to some territory so large that the friction of space is an important factor in considering the movement of commodities and personnel. Even though the regional shares may be unequal, all portions of a nation do partake of the national patrimony. Local deficiencies in goods, services, and other forms of wealth are at least partially made good by inflows from more fortunate sections. One has only to glance at such international borders as the one between Mexico and the United States to learn how different national economies create sharp differences in standards of living between two zones of quite comparable physical potentiality. Furthermore, all the raw materials need not be produced locally in order for a nation to provide adequate amounts of food, energy, clothing, and other vital necessities for its citizens; more specifically, citizens do not have to depend entirely on local resources for the jobs—and money—to purchase such items. If the nation has a large enough exportable surplus of one or more natural resources, international commerce will provide those commodities or services that are in short supply.

Obviously, the size of an area is important too. Simple territorial extent enables the United States, Australia, the Soviet Union, China, and Brazil to find within their own areas most of the natural resources they might want or need. But even with the most diligent application of known and likely techniques to, say, Switzerland, Lebanon, or Basutoland, it is impossible to envisage the local development there of most necessary foodstuffs, forest resources, minerals, energy supplies, and the like. Even though no single nation can hope to achieve total resource autarchy, relative abundance, whether bestowed by a happy coincidence of terrestrial accidents or an enormous territory, offers a degree of economic sovereignty and maneuverability that greatly facilitates the creation of a favorable population/resource ratio and hence, an adequate level of living.

The Population Factor in
the Population/Resource Ratio

A look at the resource side of the equation has shown how extremely difficult, perhaps impossible, it is to frame a realistic quantitative expression for the total resource content of any locality. But with the simple absolute population figure acting as numerator, shouldn't it be easy to insert the population factor into the ratio? Unfortunately, the problem of quantifying the human factor in the population/resource ratio is almost as delicate and bewildering as that presented by the terrestrial denominator. People are highly variable entities, not only as creators of resources, but also as customers for them. If they were no more than lumps of flesh using up fixed rations of things each day, it would only be necessary to count heads; but reality is rather more troublesome. As has been pointed out previously, a resource is an artificial construct only fractionally implicit in untampered nature. Similarly, man's appetite for most material things is only latent in human nature and must be imparted by cultural precept or commercial wheedling. If people produce wealth at unequal per capita rates in different places, they also consume things at similarly disparate rates, depending on attitude, capacity, and opportunity. For each area or community, then, one must carefully define just how much the inhabitants can and do produce *and* just how much they do or would like to consume, i.e., what an "acceptable standard of living" is considered to be, before any quantitative sense can be made of the ratio between size of resource endowment and number of people.

Obviously, below a certain level the imbalance between people and resources becomes so great that physical survival is impossible. Past this point, it is extremely difficult—for many reasons, but mainly because of intercultural differences in notions as to what constitutes poverty, a decent level of living, and affluence—to mark off absolute loci on the poverty-affluence spectrum and use them for international comparisons. Present knowledge and techniques make it difficult to go beyond such vague statements as: "There is extreme (or heavy, or moderate) pressure of population on resources"; "Population appears somewhat excessive in terms of resources"; "Population and resources seem to be well-balanced";[2] or "There is a definite (or strong, or extreme) deficiency of population with respect to resources that could be exploited with locally available techniques."

One interesting peculiarity of the population/resource ratio should be mentioned. Adding more members to the population need not neces-

[2] Although the elusive concept of an "optimum population" is in some disrepute at this time, it stubbornly refuses to die. The problem is sympathetically reviewed in Manuel Gottlieb, "The Theory of Optimum Population for a Closed Economy," *Journal of Political Economy*, Vol. 53 (December 1945), 289-316 (reprinted in Joseph J. Spengler and Otis Dudley Duncan, eds., *Population Theory and Policy: Selected Readings* (New York: Free Press of Glencoe, 1956), pp. 159-89.

sarily depress the ratio, and thus the standard of living, particularly if the people added excel the rest of the population in technical competence. When "underpopulation" prevails, any kind of population growth may well enhance the general welfare and per capita use of resources by providing labor for the efficient operation of basic economic activities. As a corollary fact, let it be noted again that simple population density must never be confused with the population/resource ratio. The statement that "x number of persons reside in y number of square kilometers" is a simple mathematical declaration with no immediate geographical implications. The only absolutely excessive physical density of population would occur in such trivial instances as the rush hour in a New York City subway car, where the absolute limits of human compressibility are achieved.

Extremely high absolute densities can coexist with inordinately high levels of income. Manhattan is an excellent illustration of this, despite its disturbingly large minority of underprivileged citizens and an obvious lack of immediate resources—aside from its transportation locus and tourist attractions. It enjoys highly favorable access to the resources of the remainder of the nation and much of the rest of the world, as expressed by the flow of funds to Manhattan and the large number of well-paying jobs locally available but ultimately based on the appropriation of resources at distant points. In highly advanced countries, severe physical congestion of populations may cause great discomfort and produce loss of efficiency, while leading at the same time to a highly desirable ratio of population to resources. (At the other extreme, many parts of the world are unable to support their small populations, despite very sparse settlement, because they lack the necessary resources to do so.) Eventually, in even the most advanced economies, it is entirely conceivable that neither the totally mobilized skills of a highly trained and elaborately equipped work force, nor the injection of huge amounts of capital, will ensure the perpetuation of adequate resources, especially if present-day population growth persists. But as yet no such situation has developed, nor does any threaten to materialize in the immediate future.

The Ackerman System of Population/Resource Regions

In view of the great difficulties involved in defining and measuring individually the resource and population factors of a region, and the equally serious problem of fitting them into a meaningful population/resource ratio, it is not surprising that the task of categorizing the world in terms of this ratio has barely been begun. The most useful such effort, and the one adopted here, is the proposal by Edward A. Ackerman for five types of population/resource regions: [3] (1) technology-

[3] "Population and Natural Resources," in Philip M. Hauser and Otis Dudley Duncan, eds., *The Study of Population: An Inventory and Appraisal* (Chicago: Univ. of Chicago, 1959), pp. 621-48.

source areas of low population-potential/resource ratio, or the *United States type;* (2) technology-source areas of high population/resource ratio, or the *European type;* (3) technology-deficient areas of low population/resource ratio, or the *Brazil type;* (4) technology-deficient areas of high population/resource ratio, or the *Egyptian type* (designated by Ackerman as the *China type,* a choice of example no longer quite as apposite as a few years ago); and (5) the *Arctic-desert type,* which is technology deficient and possesses few food-producing resources. (See Map 7 for the classification of entire nations or major portions thereof in accordance with this scheme.)

The Ackerman system, as modified here, must be regarded not as the ultimate tool in analyzing population/resource relationships, but only as a promising beginning. We lack sufficient raw data on human and physical resources and the proper scales with which to gauge them; thus this conceptual framework is at best a temporary, though serviceable, expedient. In studying any given area, the population geographer will necessarily become intimately acquainted with specific relationships between man and physical resources, both over the entirety of his study area and within more limited localities. The variety, and often uniqueness, of these localized ecological arrangements is such that no world-wide classification can be made to apply.

Of the three variables used in this scheme, the most critical would appear to be amount and quality of available technology. Where technology is highly developed and technicians are abundant, as in the United States and European types, then resources, and hence, prosperity, are at adequate, though not necessarily optimum, levels. This is true even when the national territory is cramped and the storehouse of physical resources is nearly empty. But neither small populations nor copious supplies of land and potential resources can, in themselves, make for adequate per capita levels of production and consumption. At best, they will keep the "overpopulation" of a nation under control for a certain term of years while the standard of living remains slightly above the distress level.

The United States Type

Clearly, the most enviable and exclusive regions are those that comprise the United States type. Here we find large territories well stocked with known or probable resources, populations of small or moderate size, and above all, an advanced, rapidly expanding technology, skilled personnel, and the social means for maximizing national and individual affluence.[4] By virtue of their extensive territories and general physical good fortune, these regions control domestically most of the material wherewithal necessary for a lofty social and economic estate; and their

[4] The United States type is represented in the Appendix by the United States, Canada, New Zealand, Australia, and with the qualification noted subsequently, Argentina.

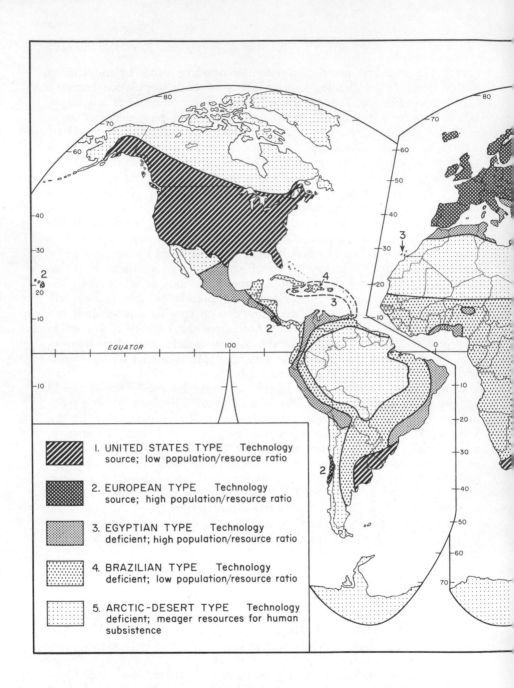

1. UNITED STATES TYPE   Technology source; low population/resource ratio

2. EUROPEAN TYPE   Technology source; high population/resource ratio

3. EGYPTIAN TYPE   Technology deficient; high population/resource ratio

4. BRAZILIAN TYPE   Technology deficient; low population/resource ratio

5. ARCTIC-DESERT TYPE   Technology deficient; meager resources for human subsistence

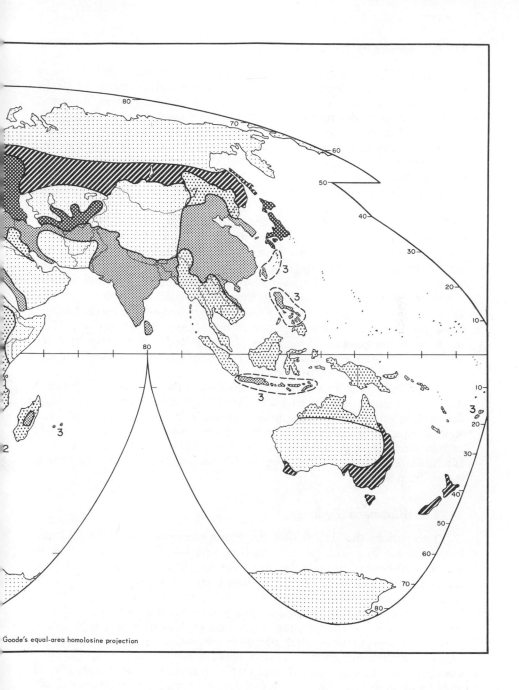

Goode's equal-area homolosine projection

7. Generalized Population/Resource Regions

external political and commercial arrangements are such that they can readily commandeer from alien sources at advantageous terms whatever else may be desired. This nearly ideal concurrence of factors is marred only by the hasty, destructive manner in which the people of these lands have handled their own (and outside) resources, especially the soils, forests and grasslands, minerals, and water supplies. The economy has developed rapidly, but possibly at the ultimate price of an irreversibly damaged habitat.

Membership in this group is limited to the United States, Canada, Australia, New Zealand, the Soviet Union (especially its more recently settled central and eastern portions), and much more dubiously, the core region of Argentina (and thus, in effect, the entire nation). Map 7 shows Uruguay and southern Brazil as United States-type regions, but only because no other category is applicable. Their qualifications are questionable—Uruguay's because of its rather modest size and limited range of resources, and southern Brazil's because the destiny of this well-favored region is so closely involved with that of the much bulkier, more problematic remainder of the nation. South Africa and the Rhodesias might be considered members of the United States group by some analysts, but their special and varied human ecologies make it impossible to classify them unequivocally.

The United States type is the most recent of the five types because it did not come into being until about 100, or at most 150, years ago when the regions listed above began to emerge from Brazilian status. But even though this system of regionalization is evolutionary, as any realistic system must be, it is highly unlikely that additional territories can join the ranks of these lucky few. The conditions for membership are simply too restrictive.

The European Type

The nations that fall within the European type must also be numbered among the élite, for the relationships between size and technological virtuosity of the population on the one hand, and the population-supporting capacities of their resources on the other, are still quite favorable, though there is much less leeway for trial and error.[5] Here a larger, denser population exploits a fund of social skills and ingenuity no less impressive, on the average, than that of United States-type lands. It must maneuver within much narrower confines of space and resources, hence, with a much more intensive local economy, and a much more conservative attitude toward renewable resources. The prosperity of such lands depends also upon an elaborate system of international ex-

[5] Several representatives of the European type listed in the Appendix, all in the "Highly Advanced" and "Advanced" sections, have excellent credentials—namely, Sweden, England and Wales, Switzerland, West Germany, Belgium, the Netherlands, France, Finland, and Japan. Poland, Hungary, and Spain can also be included, though with some hesitation. Within the "Transitional" group, Puerto Rico, Hong Kong, and Chile verge on European status.

change whereby skilled services and advanced industrial goods are traded for other such services and goods and for locally deficient fossil fuels and other minerals, forest products, foodstuffs, and unskilled or semiskilled labor. Some new local physical resources are still being found, and more significantly, new methods for extracting greater benefits from familiar resources are constantly evolving. Thus there has been a modestly successful search for additional domestic minerals, steady rises in agricultural output, a more complete realization of forest potentials, diligent cultivation of the tourist crop, further hydroelectric development, major improvements in already elaborate transportation networks, new industrial processes, and marked progress in education and modes of social organization.

Yet however intense this campaign for self-improvement may be, none of the European-type lands can escape the limitations of large populations and small territories. The near autarchy of the United States-type lands is beyond their grasp, and they are compelled to resort to vigorous international symbiosis of indefinite duration in order to survive and prosper. Not only will close trading ties have to be maintained with those "underdeveloped" lands having disposable surpluses of raw materials and labor, but there will also have to be close collaboration among the European-type nations themselves—a process that finds its highest expression in the recent appearance of the various Western European economic consortia. European-type lands should be of special interest to the population geographer, for they foreshadow the sort of crowded, intricately geared way of life that, at the moment, appears to be the only tolerable one to which the entire population of this planet can aspire. The conditions for admission to the European group of population/resource regions are less discouraging than those set for the United States group. The nations of Western, and more recently southern and Eastern, Europe have moved upward into their present category only within the past two centuries from what appears to have been Brazilian or Egyptian conditions or various intermediate forms. The boundaries of the category are fluid, and it is only with much hesitation that southern Iberia is shown as "European" in Map 7 and that Rumania, Bulgaria, Turkey, and southern Yugoslavia are excluded for the time being. Quite recently, the mass arrival of European migrants and capital has propelled such areas as Soviet Central Asia and Israel upward into the European realms. (Central Costa Rica and Chile are classed as "European" by default; their technological levels may be too low, whatever the ethnic affiliation of their citizens.) In the case of Japan, an amazing developmental program has recently lifted that nation to European status; and other Egyptian-type lands such as China, India, North Korea, Turkey, Mexico, Puerto Rico, and Ghana have exerted themselves in this direction but still remain far short of their goals. It is reasonable to expect that many more nations currently typed as Egyptian or Brazilian will apply shortly for admission to the European category, spurred on either by internal social ferment and idealistic leaderships, as in Mexico, or because of some sudden windfall additions to their resource inventory, as has occurred in Iraq and Libya with their newly found petroleum wealth.

The Brazilian Type

Among technologically deficient lands, the Brazilian type is the most fortunate—in terms of prospects if not necessarily in the current ratio between population and *developed* resources.[6] These are the areas, usually fairly substantial in size, where for a variety of cultural and historical reasons the size of present-day populations stands well below the level that could be supported comfortably with known resources, and where much larger populations could be achieved, given a higher phase of socioeconomic development. Their present status is a transient one. Almost without exception, the populations of these lands are growing rapidly, so that they will be transformed shortly into either crowded Egyptian-type countries or, given some rapid forcing of their socioeconomic adolescence, into European-type lands. There is no acute sense of pressure of man upon the land or social resources in these areas as yet, but standards of living generally fall far below levels considered acceptable by the United States- and European-type countries. Methods of resource management vary widely, from the most prodigally wasteful to the most carefully controlled, making it impossible to generalize on this point. Unlike the Egyptian-type lands, these territories have been granted a temporary reprieve from the inevitable burden of an oversized population; a cushion of space and resources affords some freedom of decision.

Most Brazilian-type lands are grouped into three large regional categories: Indochinese, or Malaysian; tropical African; and Latin American. All the territories in the Indochinese Peninsula and Greater Malaysia, with the exception of North Vietnam, the central and northern Philippines, and Java and the islands immediately to the east thereof, have population densities well below the saturation point. Although the physical resources of this large region could support much more highly developed human societies than now prevail there, formidable political and social barriers block advancement. The results would be uncertain if any of the governments concerned were to marshal their energies for a major development program, but this is something that has not yet come to pass. In nearby northern Australia, where the population potential is almost completely unrealized, there has as yet been little incentive of any kind to promote the regional economy.

Much of tropical Africa can be considered "underpopulated," but many physical as well as social problems must be vanquished before massive socioeconomic development can be realized. In the meantime,

[6] The clearest examples of Brazilian-type countries in the Appendix are Panama, Brazil (at least in part), British Guiana, the Dominican Republic, Ghana, and Angola. Major portions of Peru, Nigeria, and Kenya can also be regarded as "Brazilian."

enough detailed data and a map of larger scale than Map 7, would make it obvious that many small, but ominous, blisters of overpopulation have already erupted in a continental expanse where average population/resource pressures are still tolerably low.

Within South America, the considerable economic potentialities of the lightly peopled interior of the Brazilian Plateau and the richly endowed montaña belt flanking the eastern slope of the Andes from Bolivia to Venezuela are being exploited by migrants newly arrived from more crowded regions; but this is often done in such a haphazard way that the *whole* of the nation may not be propelled upward on the socioeconomic ladder. In interior Argentina and in the entirety of Paraguay, however, many decades will pass before a sizeable economic potential can be either ruined or properly nurtured. The sparsely occupied lowlands along the northwestern margin of South America (and eastern Panama), from the Gulf of Darien to the Gulf of Guayaquil, have possibilities that can be realized only quite slowly because of both physical and social hindrances. Rapid internal growth in the Guianas threatens to consume in a short time the excess of known resources available until recently to a scant population.

Other isolated pockets of Brazilian-type country remain to be mentioned: The Caribbean flank (and much of the Pacific littoral) of Central America, Cuba, and the Dominican Republic could absorb a considerable addition of people if a more efficient developmental system than is now at hand were available. Iraq, with its ample soil, water, and petroleum resources, gives great promise for future evolution; similar possibilities exist in Kuwait, Bahrein, and other Persian Gulf principalities, though they are endowed with scarcely anything beyond bountiful petroleum and natural gas reserves. The relatively uncrowded, but attractively equipped, Manchurian and North Korean regions have been the objects of intensive Japanese, Russian, and Chinese interest and already seem well on their way up from Brazilian status.

The Egyptian Type

The fourth of our population/resource categories, the Egyptian, is most discouraging in its imbalance of excessive numbers of consumers and shortages of immediately available resources, both physical and social.[7] Membership in this group is growing more rapidly than that of any other category at the present time, virtually at a cancerous rate, and at the expense of Brazilian-type lands. These "Egyptian" lands are densely populated, not only in terms of sheer numbers, but also in ratio of inhabitants to accessible means of subsistence or employment. Excessive pressure of human beings upon physical and social resources, al-

[7] The Egyptian-type countries encountered in the Appendix include Mexico (or at least the bulk of that nation), Cyprus, El Salvador, Turkey, Jamaica, Tunisia, a good portion of Peru, the Philippines, Ceylon, the Fiji Islands, South Korea, and Pakistan. Major sections of Nigeria and Korea must also be classed as "Egyptian."

ready close to critical, and swiftly growing worse, affords scant hope for any qualitative improvement in the welfare of these groups—unless there is a revolutionary, and thus quite painful, transformation of society and economy by either external or internal forces. In some instances, the physical endowment is such that even the most radically thoroughgoing approach to a community's development would seem to offer little chance of general betterment.

In the broadest sense, most of mankind has found itself in a similar predicament at one time or another throughout most of recorded history, i.e., human needs pressing well beyond the areal and technical means of satisfaction; but it is really only in recent decades that the Egyptian type of population/resource situation can be said to have existed as a full-blown, pathological entity. Only in modern times have technologically deficient folk reached such great numbers and excessive densities; only recently have such great numbers aspired to higher levels of existence, draining their supplies of physical resources so seriously that it is often dubious whether even the most skillful, technologically advanced reordering of the economy can appease their material wants and needs. These lands are doubly stricken: Their excessive numbers confront deficient material and social capital, and their chances for escape upward to the status of European-type countries are very slim. In rare instances, such a deliverance may be possible: Puerto Rico, which enjoys a number of extraordinary advantages, seems to be making the transition; Japan, now a European-type nation, narrowly escaped Egyptian status; and China, India, and other lands are making extraordinary efforts, as yet with indeterminate results, to join the ranks of the technologically adept European lands that enjoy tolerable levels of living.

Egypt illustrates the general problems of these technologically backward countries. The ecumene of this ancient land has always been confined to the alluvial valley of the Nile. Nearly all this precious soil is given over to raising food crops for a population that is now doubling its size roughly every 25 years; only a minor fraction of it is allotted to exportable crops such as cotton. The meager store of undeveloped arable land will probably be exhausted long before the end of this century. Egypt lacks any significant untapped mineral, forest, or marine resources in addition to the large energy supplies (beyond solar energy) that are necessary for developing an industrial economy; and tourist dollars, though not to be ignored, can never become a decisive source of income. Virtually no outlets exist in other parts of the world for Egyptians who might want to emigrate, and military conquest of neighboring lands, with the dubious exception of the Sudan, would open no new horizons for colonization. Integrating the Egyptian economy with that of neighboring states, an expedient now being explored, offers only slim hope for deliverance from the population/resource crisis, since these neighbors are almost as inadequately outfitted for economic advancement as is Egypt. Equally grave—and particularly ironic in a land that was once the unquestioned leader of civilized nations—are the human and institutional barriers to general progress: the low incidence of educated and literate persons; the general absence of advanced skills; conservative, even negative, social attitudes; the present incapacity of a large peasant population for anything beyond its current hand-to-mouth existence. The one small glimmer of hope for the nation is its revenue from the Suez Canal; but as in the parallel case of Panama, this is a weak foundation upon which to build a national economy.

Egyptian-type lands are encountered on every continent, but with a decided emphasis on areas of lower latitude.[8] Other African examples are Algeria, Tunisia, and Morocco. Portions of southern Europe, particularly Sicily, Sardinia, southern Italy, Albania, Greece, and southern Yugoslavia, might be considered Egyptian; parts of Spain and Portugal have been given the benefit of doubt on Map 7 and are termed European. South of the Sahara, a number of tracts are teetering dangerously between the Brazilian and Egyptian categories, and some, e.g., Ruanda, Burundi, Basutoland, or the more congested segments of the Cameroons or Kenya, may belong to the latter. In the New World, Haiti is probably as stark an example as any of the Egyptian type of nation, with its combination of severe population pressure and sorely limited land resources. Elsewhere in the Caribbean, Jamaica and nearly all the Lesser Antilles must be classed as members of the Egyptian group. On the mainland, El Salvador, much of upland Guatemala, and (with less certainty) the bulk of Mexico fall into the same class. In South America, "Egyptian" must be applied to much of the Andean highland country, from Ecuador (or possibly Colombia) to Bolivia and quite emphatically to northeast Brazil. Asia holds the great majority of the people consigned to this least desirable population/resource situation. China occupies a somewhat anomalous position at the moment, but most of the country must still be categorized as Egyptian; and the same holds true for the huge Indian and Pakistani populations. Elsewhere along the Asian periphery, South Korea, Taiwan, North Vietnam, Luzon and some of the Visayan Group, Java and Timor along with the isles in between, Ceylon, Syria, Lebanon, Cyprus, and Jordan all bear the Egyptian label. A number of other Asian territories, such as Nepal, Afghanistan, Iran, and portions of Turkey, are difficult to classify (in part, for sheer lack of data) and might be regarded as either Brazilian or Egyptian in character. The great majority of inhabited islands within the Pacific Basin are of the Javanese type, despite the small absolute sizes of their

[8] It is tempting, but unwise, to look for some cause-and-effect relationship between tropical location and the Egyptian population/resource situation. There is no valid case for a tropical environment as a prime genetic factor per se; rather, a complex web of historic, and probably temporary, happenstance has brought about a grouping of demographic and economic "problem areas" in the tropics. Before A.D. 1200, the relative status of the middle-latitude vs. the low-latitude lands was quite the opposite of what it is today. Brian J. L. Berry analyzes this phenomenon in "Basic Patterns of Economic Development," in Norton Ginsburg, *Atlas of Economic Development* (Chicago: Univ. of Chicago, 1961), pp. 110-19.

populations; the same observation applies to a number of islands in the Indian and Atlantic oceans, such as Mauritius, Réunion, the Canaries, and the Azores.

The Arctic-Desert Type

The population/resource category of least direct concern to the population geographer is the Arctic-desert type; it includes all those fairly extensive areas that for reasons of aridity, cold, inaccessible terrain, remoteness, or other physical impediments are entirely unsettled, only intermittently occupied, or at best, the homes of small, marginal groups. Although it is possible that unforeseen technological developments may render some of these areas quite tenable, for the present, their value lies in the abundant supply of raw materials—mineral ores and fuels, furs, marine life, and hydroelectric power. In addition to the scattered groups of usually transient personnel exploiting these resources, and the small bands of hunters, pastoralists, or cultivators ekeing out a bare existence in relatively favored tracts, the only other inhabitants would be military and scientific workers and some hardy tourists and sportsmen. A genuine population problem cannot be said to exist in such territories since, in the event of any calamity, their residents can, and usually do, take refuge in more habitable areas.

All of Antarctica (along with the sub-Antarctic islands) and Greenland are emphatically "Arctic-desert." The greater part of northern North America, much of northern Eurasia, and the archipelagoes to the north of these continental masses must clearly be put into the same category, and the same holds true for the vast region comprising the Sahara and the drier stretches of Southwest and Central Asia. Among the smaller occurrences of this type are the nearly empty sections of north-central and northwest Mexico and the southwest United States, the coastal desert of Peru and north Chile (omitting the permanent oases, of course), much of Amazonia, most of Patagonia, Central Australia, and the bleaker reaches of Southwest Africa. In a sense, the great oceanic expanses might also be included in this company. Much animal food and some plant life, in addition to an increasing quantity of minerals, is extracted from the sea, and there are serious future possibilities for some forms of crop and livestock cultivation; but until now, the seas have been tenanted only by small, roving groups of land-based harvesters.

CHAPTER TWELVE

Population/resource regions

The United States Type:
The Canadian Example

The potentialities of this fourfold approach to the study of population geography can be made more clear by selecting an example of each of the four permanently inhabited types of population/resource regions and tracing out its profile in terms of the proposed classification. Let us choose Canada as an example of the United States type.[1]

What is Canada's cultural identity? Ignoring the numerically insignificant aboriginal survivors, the nation is unmistakably European in character; more specifically, it is a pairing of the British and French cultures, the former being in much the superior position. This British Canadian culture (with recognizable Scotch and Scotch-Irish strains) has, like the cultures of the United States, Australia, New Zealand, and South Africa, undergone a change brought about by the impact of a novel physical environment, unfamiliar social and economic conditions, and some interchange with aboriginal groups and immigrants from other parts of the world. Although Canada is primarily British in character, a colonial, specifically, American accent is present, with all the demographic postulates implied thereby; but the admission of considerable numbers of newcomers from Germany, Scandinavia, Ireland, the Nether-

---

[1] Major aspects of Canada's geography and population are dealt with in Griffith Taylor, *Canada: A Study of Cool Environments and Their Effect on British and French Settlement,* 2nd ed. (New York: Dutton, 1950) (tendentious, but useful); Canada, Department of Mines and Surveys, Geography Branch, *Atlas of Canada* (Ottawa, 1957); and Paul Veyret, *La Population du Canada* (Paris: Presses Univ. de France, 1953). The statistics cited for Canada in the Appendix are also useful in this discussion.

lands, Poland, Russia, Italy, and elsewhere has not been without some effects upon the British majority. The nature of this dominant British-Canadian culture, though quite accessible to study, has not been fully charted, nor have some of the significant current changes been fully appreciated. Consequently, we are by no means adequately equipped to evaluate its demographic implications.

The French Canadian group has remained strongly immiscible, both socially and territorially, relative to British and other populations. (It has also diverged sharply from the mother country in its demographic career.) Since it forms some 30 per cent of the aggregate population and is sharply segregated areally, the distinct demographic differences between this large French minority and the rest of the nation are of considerable geographic interest. Although certain fundamental, basically British, traits appear in the emerging pan-Canadian national culture, one can also detect significant regional deviations. Newfoundland's or New Brunswick's English-speaking citizens do not follow quite the same patterns of thought or behavior as the people in southern Ontario or those in Alberta; but taken as a whole, these differences are fewer and less pronounced than might be expected over such vast distances.

What of the level of Canada's socioeconomic structure? Again, ignoring the Indians and Eskimos who sparsely occupy so large a portion of the nation's territory, Canada is clearly one of the most advanced representatives of "occidental urban civilization," a fact setting off limitless reverberations in its demography and population geography. The most intense phase of this socioeconomic system, a highly complex urban-industrial culture, is limited largely to portions of southern Quebec and Ontario. Elsewhere, the continuously settled land is given over mainly to commercial agriculture and widely spaced urban trade, transport, and processing centers, and its margins to forestry, fishing, and mining; but the whole of this ecumene is powerfully integrated into the economic heartland of Anglo-America. This advanced form of economic production and distribution and of spatial integration is closely intertwined with the areal patterns of population characteristics and change; the areal shape of the economic system relates closely to the highly dynamic, economically sensitive population. Age and sex, fertility, sex ratio, occupation, income, educational attainment, migratory history—all these and many other population traits are spatially closely associated with the workings of the economic system.

Canada's shifting relations with the outer world have been most interesting. From a position of provincial, almost total reliance upon Great Britain, in terms of migrants, ideas, trade, and political power, Canada has grown into a cosmopolitan nation of considerable autonomy. The connection with Great Britain has been nominally preserved, more strongly through the bonds of sentiment than by the last flimsy fibers of political attachment; but Canada now transmits as well as receives educational, scientific, and artistic cargo from the outer world. It has evolved from an exclusive exporter of raw materials to a merchandiser of industrial products and investment capital. In addition, Canada is one of the few countries still accepting large numbers of immigrants, mostly from the United Kingdom and continental Europe, but always on Canadian terms. Great Britain's parental role has been usurped by the United States to a remarkable degree. Indeed, in many ways the two countries are almost symbiotically fused, so much so that certain parts of Canada may sometimes feel a closer affinity with their sister regions across the border than with distant, dissimilar parts of Canada. Many Canadians believe that their national integrity is being gravely threatened by the colossus to the south, but in any event, the mass exchange of visitors, goods, services, and ideas between the two nations continues; and this intimate liaison is a paramount fact in Canadian population geography.

The economically potent southern fringe of Canada is decidedly an example of the United States population/resource region. This is the dominant fact despite the enormous expanse of Arctic and sub-Arctic land that must be classed "Arctic-desert," and the marginal character of Newfoundland and portions of Quebec and the Maritime Provinces that might just as readily be called "European" in terms of population/resource relations. And of course this statement implies for Canada an enviably spacious, comfortable set of economic and demographic alternatives in its future evolution. Keeping the foregoing facts in mind, the student is prepared not only to approach Canadian population geography as an isolated phenomenon, but also to make fruitful comparisons with cognate communities; in every major respect, except for the uniqueness of the French Canadian group and the peculiarities of the bonds with the United States, Canadians do resemble several other population groups in other parts of the world.

The European Type: The Netherlands Example

Let us employ the Netherlands as an example of the European type of population/resource situation.[2] The Dutch are decidedly members of the large European community of cultures, and in language and other respects are close cousins of the British—and thus, by extension, of the Canadians—and of the neighboring Flemish and Germans. Yet here, certainly, a distinctive national culture is in evidence. The Dutch linguistic area is virtually coincident with the national boundaries, except for those speakers of the language that are in present or former colonies—unless one regards Flemish as an identical language. Less overt elements of thought and behavior to which the experienced observer would be sensitive also distinguish the Dutch from other Europeans.

[2] Pertinent data are available for the Netherlands in the Appendix. Important background material on the country can be found in Albert Demangeon, "Les Pays-Bas," in *Géographie Universelle*, II (Paris: Colin, 1927), 156-237, and Bartholomew Landheer, ed., *The Netherlands*, United Nations Series (Berkeley and Los Angeles: Univ. of California, 1943).

Within the nation, there are remnants of regional cultures (and dialects) that have persisted for centuries, as well as the nearly universal cultural dichotomy between city and countryside or the differentiations along class lines. Within the larger cities, as befits their cosmopolitan status, there have been small groups of immigrants from other European lands and from overseas, and until World War II, a significant number of Jews. To the population scientist, however, a near numerical balance between the two large religious communities—Protestant and Roman Catholic—has been a particularly crucial cultural fact to consider in the Netherlands. This fact has had a serious impact upon the social and political life of the nation and, evidently, upon its demographic behavior as well. Many observers attribute the unusually high fertility of the Dutch—high at least by Northwest European standards—and a bumper crop of babies this densely crowded land can ill afford, to the latent hostility of the two groups, a kind of "battle of the cradle."

In the socioeconomic sphere, the Netherlands is an excellent example of "occidental urban civilization" and is indeed part of the zone in which this climactic form of human society was incubated. This is borne out by the high percentage of urban population (88 per cent in parishes with more than 5,000 inhabitants); intense industrial and commercial development; the extraordinary, but specialized, pursuit of agriculture; and the age, income, educational, and occupational structure of the population. The high socioeconomic status of the Dutch is attested to by various demographic indices; in some, such as infant mortality or life expectation at birth, the Netherlands has reached a level not exceeded elsewhere. This status has for the Dutch all the demographic concomitants found in similar communities, plus others created by unique historical, locational, and physical facts.

The external relations of the Netherlands have not only been exceptionally varied and interesting but have also been utterly essential to the nation's survival and prosperity. In ancient times, this area lay at the outermost limits of the known world and it enters history as one of the marchlands of the Roman Empire. In subsequent centuries, the Netherlands played a rather passive role until its sudden emergence from Spanish rule followed by its expansion into a leading naval and mercantile power in the sixteenth century. Both before and after that period, a complex exchange of ideas and influences, as well as commerce and services, has taken place, not only with Spain but also with Great Britain, France, Germany, and the United States, to cite only the major partners. A period of more than three centuries as a major colonial power has left important traces on the present-day country. Temporary holdings in North America, Ceylon, East Asia, Brazil, and South Africa and the more enduring occupance of Surinam, the Netherlands Antilles, and above all, the East Indies, meant important flows of population and wealth between metropolis and colony. Relatively small numbers of Dutch emigrated to the Americas, but there were significant contributions to the populations of South Africa and Indonesia.

Today, however, these overseas contingents of Dutch are of no consequence to the motherland. The Boers were cut adrift early, both socially and politically, and their present orphaned status is closely analagous to the Quebec-France situation; and virtually the whole European cohort in Indonesia has been repatriated in recent years. Continuous emigration is one of the devices whereby a threat to the economic well-being of the country is prevented from materializing. It is within the commercial realm, however, that its ties with the outer world have been paramount for the past four centuries. Because of a position at the entrance to the greatest trade route in Europe, and because of the initiative of its citizens, the Netherlands enjoys, and is, in fact, utterly dependent upon, a vigorous continental and overseas commerce. This role as middleman for much of Western and Central Europe overshadows all else in the economic and population geography of the Dutch. An impressive industrial superstructure and recent progress toward the integration of Western Europe have confirmed this position.

The Netherlands offers as extreme an example of the European type of population/resource situation as one could hope to find. A large, dense, healthy, thrifty, highly skilled and educated, elaborately regimented population, rich in managerial talent and entrepreneurial drive, inhabits a relatively tiny, indifferently endowed territory. In spite of superb achievements in wresting greater and greater yields from a grudging soil— and despite the polderization of coastal waters and an access to the rich fishing grounds of the North Sea—the Netherlands can never hope to nourish its present or future inhabitants without heavy imports of foodstuffs for both people and livestock. Similarly, the Dutch factories must rely on foreign areas for critical raw materials as well as for much of their market. They operate in a land that has only modest coal deposits and, despite the recent discovery of Europe's greatest natural gas field, has a total package of raw materials quite inadequate to the needs of an important industrial nation. These limitations of the land are such that rapid developments in the fields of commerce, industry, transport, and other services will be needed to maintain or raise present levels of living. Unabated growth of population, plus the repatriation of large numbers of overseas Dutch, makes the problem even more difficult to solve. Such a categorization, brief as it is, should precede a study of the population geography of the Netherlands.

The Brazilian Type:
The Example of British Guiana

Much greater diversity of culture, economic form, and man-land relationships is found in the communities of the Brazilian or Egyptian types, and here the search for analogous situations becomes more difficult. In the case of British Guiana, the Brazilian type used here, useful parallels can be found only in its immediate neighbors, Surinam and

French Guiana.[3] Before the coast of British Guiana enjoyed the cursory attention of the Spanish and then partial occupation by the Dutch, it was sparsely settled by some of the more primitive aboriginal groups of South America, who combined desultory farming with hunting and gathering. The small size of this native population seems to have been the result of two factors: the terminal, "dead-end" position of British Guiana with respect to aboriginal sources of cultural innovation and hence, a relative backwardness; and the mediocrity of most of the land for agricultural or wild food production. Three centuries of contact with outsiders have badly decimated the aborigines. It appears unlikely that they can ever recover their original numbers or exert much cultural influence on the well-settled areas.

It is to the immigrant groups, then, that one must look for British Guiana's cultural identity. Relatively few Dutch (a number of them Jews by way of Brazil) or later, British, were ever domiciled in British Guiana; but their effects upon the economy and many aspects of the general culture have been decisive. Still, it would be misleading to label British Guiana as more than fractionally European in culture. The African slaves and their descendants (Creoles), who, until recently, formed the great preponderance of British Guianans, represent a wide assortment of African stocks, though most of them come from the Guinea Coast. How much of their original culture survived the trauma of capture, transatlantic passage, and prolonged enslavement is still uncertain; but some residue of the African pattern continues to exist. In any event, the Negroid population has only selectively absorbed European traits. The few communities of Bush Negroes—escaped slaves—are far less numerous than they are in Surinam; but as is the case there, retention of Africanisms has been relatively great.

The East Indian population, introduced by the British in response to persistent labor shortages after the emancipation of the Negro slaves, kept a good deal of its original culture intact. After an initial period during which individuals lost their ties to villages or larger communities, the East Indians managed to crystallize a new society, one unmistakably based on traditional models despite gross alterations. Since the East Indian and Creole populations are now roughly equal in numbers and adhere to quite distinct cultures, between which there is only slight interchange, British Guiana can be held up as a clear example of a plural society. The constant cultural tension between the two dominant groups is a dominating factor in the political, social, economic, and demographic behavior of the country. Other groups—the aborigines, Bush Negroes, and British already mentioned, and some Chinese, Levantines, Portuguese, and miscellaneous Europeans and mixed-bloods—are small in number, though not necessarily in economic significance. Although there is

    [3] See David Lowenthal, "Population Contrasts in the Guianas," *Geographical Review,* Vol. 50, No. 1 (January 1960), 41-58 and Irene B. Taeuber, "British Guiana: Some Demographic Aspects of Economic Development," *Population Index,* Vol. 18, No. 1 (January 1952), 3-10.

much overlap between the two large Negro and East Indian groups in economic status and occupational structure, their cultures are strikingly different, as are their demographic patterns. These differences are matters of surpassing importance to the population student, for they create and maintain divergent population geographies for the two groups no matter how the subject is approached—whether through numbers and distribution, residence, marital structure, fertility, rate of change, age, or any other demographic element.

Excluding the interior, which must be categorized as an area of clan peasantry, British Guiana remains a plantation country in a socioeconomic sense. Even though slavery was legally abolished in the 1830's, the plantation economy and the aftereffects of slavery continue to permeate the life of the country, as has been the case in so many other Caribbean lands. In this one dimension, at least, there is a close demographic correspondence between British Guiana and other areas indelibly marked by the plantation slavery economy. The occidental urban civilization has not yet arrived here—and may never do so; so far, it has affected British Guiana only in a marginal manner.

In its external relations, British Guiana has, until recently, shown all the earmarks of a colonial territory. As noted above, most of the population, except for the small plantocracy and commercial élite, was introduced through various forms of coercion. In recent decades, much attention has been given to the possibilities of settling additional immigrants in British Guiana, specifically European refugees, or surplus populations from the British West Indies; but no practical action has been taken. On the other hand, the Guianans, less troubled by population pressures than other groups, have not availed themselves as freely of the migrational opportunities offered by Great Britain as have the Jamaicans or Barbadians. And so for the past few decades, the net flow of migrants has been insignificant.

In terms of both ideas and economic transactions, British Guiana has remained passive. Great Britain has contributed more than any other source: despite a limited degree of political sovereignty, the government is still under British supervision; British education and British ideals in general have no competitors among the more advanced strata of society; and Great Britain still accounts for much of the country's trade. Quite recently, though, some reorientation of the pattern of external connection has been brought about by the advent of heavy American and Canadian capial investment and a large outflow of raw materials to North America. On the other hand, one must note the surprising weakness of ties of any sort with the neighboring Guianas or with the Antilles. Locally, this disjointed state of affairs at the macroregional level is mirrored by quite defective physical and social communications among the various coastal settlements.

The nature of the land and its people clearly consigns British Guiana to the ranks of the Brazilian-type countries. A largely agrarian population with few skills and meager education, low income, inadequate capital, ineffective social or economic organization, and only a weak impulse toward a loftier estate inhabits a land that appears capable of supporting far more people at a much higher level. Even the agricultural sector holds vast opportunities for progress. A large part of the potentially productive coastal plain is unused, partly through absence of population pressure, more often for lack of the capital and personnel required for major reclamation and drainage works. But even within areas that are presently being cultivated, considerable improvements in land management, yields, and profits could be effected. Coastal British Guiana might, with proper handling, become a prosperous provider of foodstuffs for its own rapidly increasing citizenry, and an exporter of the same staples to the Antilles and of tropical specialties to the nontropical world. So far there has not been even a pretense of using the food resources of the coastal waters.

The large interior has little land suitable for cultivation or for effective farming of any kind; but again, with proper management and input of capital, the savannas could support much larger and better herds of cattle than they now do. Those vast interior tracts suited for neither field nor pasture may hold interesting prospects for commercial forestry—with careful experimentation, planning, and management—and the export of timber to a growing, insatiable world market. The geological exploration of the interior is incomplete, but a number of major ore bodies are known to exist and could be exploited in the fairly near future. The immense hydroelectric potential of the interior that is yet to be tapped could furnish limitless cheap energy for whatever industrial development occurs in British Guiana. Taken together, such a set of resources offers the Guianans considerable scope for economic progress—but progress will have to be made if trouble is to be averted. Pockets of overpopulation and underemployment are already sporadically visible along the coast; and given the rapid rate of population increase and the slow pace of economic advance, it is not inconceivable that in the absence of a determined development program, British Guiana might well slide downward in a few decades into the ranks of the Egyptian-type countries.

The Egyptian Type:
The South Korean Example

The Republic of Korea (South Korea) is one of the more characteristic representatives of those unfortunate lands that are classed as Egyptian-type population/resource groups and whose population problems seem particularly disturbing.[4] North Korea is excluded from this discus-

[4] Korea's population is treated in Irene B. Taeuber, "Korea in Transition: Demographic Aspects," *Population Index*, Vol. 10 (1944), 229-42 and "The Population Potential of Postwar Korea," *Far Eastern Quarterly*, Vol. 5 (1945-46), 289-307, and Glenn T. Trewartha and Wilbur Zelinsky, "Population Distribution and Change in Korea, 1925-1949," *Geographical Review*, Vol. 45, No. 1 (1955), 1-26. For a more comprehensive treatment of Korean geography and economy, see Hoon K. Lee, *Land Utilization and Rural Economy in Korea* (Chicago: Institute for Pacific Relations, 1936); A. J. Grajdanzev, *Modern Korea* (New York: Institute for Pacific Relations,

sion, partly because it is at best a marginal example of the Egyptian type (and is closer to the Brazilian classification), but especially since the events of the past 20 years have caused its society, economy, and so presumably its demography to diverge greatly from South Korea's. The general cultural identity of the Koreans is easy to establish (though their ultimate origins are quite obscure), for they are members of that large segment of mankind whose culture is designated as Sino-Japanese. The unusual degree of isolation that Korea has experienced for so long has, however, ensured a distinct personality and homogeneity for its culture, notably its language. This culture, which is virtually coextensive with the national territory, if we include North Korea, was formed largely from elements received from China, and probably Northeast Asia, perhaps 2,000 to 3,000 years ago. One of the important economic characteristics Korea shares with kindred cultures—one of special meaning to the population geographer—is the major emphasis on wet rice and other irrigated crops, a horticultural approach to land-use, and thus a close association between population density and well-being on the one hand, and the supply of alluvial land, warmth, and rainfall on the other. Korea, like China and Japan, has been the seat of a high civilization, with all that that implies in terms of government, science, the arts, and gracious living—at least for the fortunate few.

In socioeconomic terms, Korea exemplifies an "urban civilization of the rent-capitalist type," a system that, no doubt, reached the country by way of China. Quite recently, Japanese and American proddings have caused some faint beginnings of occidental urban civilization to appear in the larger cities; but South Korea is demographically still very much a peasant society (subspecies Sino-Japanese) upon which a few provincial cities and a small middle and upper class have been grafted. If the residential, occupational, educational, age, migrational, fertility, and mortality characteristics of South Korea were to be reviewed, they would be found to fall close to the modal values for all such existing societies.

Korea's nickname, the "Hermit Kingdom," has not been undeserved. After the early period of receptivity to Chinese influences and the export of Chinese and Korean culture elements to the Japanese archipelago,

1944); and Shannon McCune, *Korea's Heritage: A Regional and Social Geography* (Rutland: Tuttle, 1956).

    Since South Korea is so nearly ideal an example of the Egyptian type of population/resource situation, a note may be in order here on the literature covering the more general problem of "overpopulation"—the growing disparity between human numbers and means of subsistence in many parts of the contemporary world. Among the more alarmist book-length statements are William Vogt, *Road to Survival* (New York: Sloane, 1948) and Fairfield Osborn, ed., *Our Crowded Planet: Essays on the Pressures of Population* (Garden City: Doubleday, 1962). For more temperate, but still quite sobering, accounts of the population problem, see Political and Economic Planning, *World Population and Resources. A Report by PEP* (London: Allen, 1955); Roy G. Francis, ed., *The Population Ahead* (Minneapolis: Univ. of Minnesota, 1958); J. O. Hertzler, *The Crisis in World Population. A Sociological Examination with Special Reference to the Underdeveloped Areas* (Lincoln: Univ. of Nebraska, 1956); Philip M. Hauser, ed., *The Population Dilemma* (Englewood Cliffs: Prentice-Hall, 1963). A Spectrum Book.

Korea remained almost hermetically sealed from the outer world despite episodes of nominal Chinese suzerainty. In recent decades, the country has served as a buffer between Russia, Japan, China, and the United States; but the most serious alien effects were those brought about by Japan during its 40 years of occupation when the economic life of Korea and all its foreign relations were directed from Tokyo, and a considerable contingent of Japanese was dispatched to Korea. American influences were important even before the Japanese conquest through the vigorous work of church missionaries; since 1945, South Korea has maintained close military and economic bonds with the United States.

The Korean population is notable for its ethnic uniformity; since the expulsion of the Japanese, non-Korean elements have amounted to far less than one per cent of the total population. The in-gathering of emigrant Koreans after World War II or the flight of many North Koreans to the South did nothing, of course, to dilute this homogeneity. The labor migration of Koreans to Japan that reached large proportions before World War II has resumed in recent years; but Koreans have had much less success in migrating to other lands in East Asia or to the Americas. (It must be assumed that the rather substantial movement of Koreans to Manchuria and the Soviet Far East originated almost wholly from present-day North Korea.) Except for the political, demographic, and commercial connections with Japan and the United States and restricted intercourse with other nations, Korea's external relations have not had much impact upon the nation; one need not be too concerned with the outer world in treating Korea's population geography.

The reasons for assigning South Korea to the Egyptian group are painfully clear: The population suffers from most of the same disabilities as British Guiana, with the unwelcome addition of the effects of a disastrous war and political instability. A considerable amount of American aid and investment has not yet been able to do away with the immemorial stagnation of Korean society and economy or to set the nation on the path toward a higher level of existence. It is doubtful if Korea's social capital, whether measured in terms of education, skills, or aspiration, is sufficient to handle the task at this time. In addition, the arable lands (and offshore marine resources) of the country are already intensively developed, with a large amount of rural underemployment already in evidence; and the limits to which per unit productivity can be pushed under present conditions are not too far off. Nonagricultural economic possibilities are quite limited: There is little undeveloped mineral wealth or hydroelectric potential (in contrast to North Korea); the forest resource is of no great consequence; and without the massive introduction of foreign capital and raw materials, it will be extremely difficult to generate any important new manufacturing industries. All the while, of course, the rate of population growth has not diminished, and a doubling of the Korean population in 25 or 30 years seems likely. It is a grim background, but a necessary one, against which to mount a study of Korean population geography.

CHAPTER THIRTEEN

A final word

Approaching the Study of Population Regions: A Summary

These, then, are four examples of an experimental typology of population regions. In each case, the same four fundamental questions have been posed in preparation for close examination of the immediate facts of population: (1) Who are these people, and what is their culture like? (2) What kind of an economy do they have, and at what stage of socioeconomic advancement is it? (3) What kinds of relationships do they have with other peoples and areas? (4) In what kind of population/resource situation do they find themselves? A fifth problem, the dimension of time and change, envelops all of these: How, in what direction, and how rapidly are these phenomena being modified? Ultimately, all four dimensions in this scheme merge into a tightly interlaced whole, no part of which can vary without some important warping of the other dimensions. The scheme is not in itself a recipe for the formulation of research in population geography; it simply provides the necessary background for such research (and as noted before, for research in many other branches of geography).

We have no simple answers to the simple questions: "Why do people live where they do?" or "What are the differences in populations from place to place?" He who seeks meaningful answers commits himself to absorbing the full array of demographic facts about the community, its economy, its social fabric, its physical surroundings, its history. The areal facts of population are so closely orchestrated with the totality of geographic reality that the only prudent approach to their study presupposes a scholarly methodology taking this totality into account. Since the active agent here—in process, in space, in time—is the society itself, we must begin by understanding it thoroughly, first its essential nature—the interior, peculiar, private world of its culture—and secondly, its outward dealings with the earth—the livelihood pattern, the social machinery, the interplay with the physical milieu, all the strands of thought, action, and substance that weave this society into the lives of people both near and far.

The precise procedures to be followed in any specific research venture depend upon the purposes of the work, the nature and extent of the region or population being dealt with, the kinds of information available, and the scope of the study, i.e., whether it is to be a full-scale treatment of population phenomena or simply some limited aspects. In any event, it seems logical for the investigator to work out the placement of his study area with reference to the four elements of this typology if he is to provide himself with essential perspective and depth of understanding.[1] Only after becoming sensitized to the cultures he is dealing with, their socioeconomic configurations, and their long-distance linkages, and only after he learns a good deal about their resource ecology is the student ready to reach out and ask the question that has no final, absolute answer but like all valid geographic mysteries must be posed again and again: In what ways do areal variations in population relate to the total nature of places?

Looking Further Afield

This proposed methodology strongly emphasizes the most meaningful possible description and classification of entire regions and communities —the importance of seeing populations whole. Learning where different kinds of people live leads inevitably into a comprehensive approach to the entire range of geography and the nature of society, and into many neighboring studies. An approach like this is obviously useful in dealing with regions in their entirety and in accounting for the full range of their demographic contents as they appear in space and time. But the same fourfold classification is equally valid in coping with more restricted topics: If we describe and explain the patterns of population distribution in, say, Korea, the immediate physical, economic, general cultural, and specific political factors that impinge on fertility, mortality, and migration, and thus, in turn, on the number and location of people, will make

---

[1] The mechanics of this preparatory exercise need not always be laid bare; their effects will be implicit in the final results and will redound their benefit. For example, a population geographer analyzing some aspect of the population of the United States for an audience of Americans would do well to review his notions about the basic demographic personality of the American nation in the light of the foregoing scheme, no matter how prosaically familiar the region may seem. The unexpected sidelights shed on, say, the Middle West by this preliminary effort may be somewhat disconcerting but they will make for a richer, more meaningful product—even if the writer does not spell out in full his new insights. If this typology, or hopefully, some improvement upon it, can be useful in dealing with the familiar, it should prove indispensable in approaching unfamiliar peoples and places.

much more sense if we know as much as possible about the cultural identity and character of Korea, its level and pace of socioeconomic development, its connections with other parts of the world, and its population-technology-resource budget. The same observation would apply equally well to an analysis of ethnic groups in British Guiana, the geography of age groups in Canada, or spatial patterns of urbanization in the Netherlands.

For lack of space, too little attention has been given to the interplay among two or more sets of population phenomena. Obviously, a considerable part of the total population geography of any area can be attributed to these quite numerous intramural interactions within the bounds of demography. How are the spatial patterns of urbanization related to ethnic patterns in British Guiana? What sorts of areal variations are there in the relationships between fertility and population density in South Korea? What are the mutual effects of age structure, sex, and occupation in different parts of Canada? What are the relationships between migrational events and urban-rural residence in the various regions of the Netherlands? These questions, and many more like them, can be pursued more effectively when the student has gained perspective on the countries involved by viewing them in the light of the typology suggested here.

The final, and perhaps most important item on the agenda of the population geographer, is the study of the effects of population phenomena, and particularly change, upon the nondemographic phases of geography. Little has as yet been done in this direction, but it is safe to predict that geographers will soon become immersed in such problems as how population structure and dynamics act differently in different places to affect habitat and resources; how the population factor reacts upon the economic behavior of a community and, particularly, the type and direction of its current economic development; its impact upon the political and other aspects of social geography; and the effects of changing population characteristics upon the basic structure of the total culture.

Along with other social scientists, the geographer will be called upon to study the problems of population growth and rate of change, and the stresses imposed upon society and habitat by enormous increases in human numbers and appetites—practical and theoretical challenges of a completely new order of magnitude. Whether or not mankind successfully meets the crises of the current demographic and technological revolutions, the next several decades will certainly be a dangerous, tension-ridden period, one of great intellectual excitement and major progress in population science.

Selected references

The following list includes important references and substantive works that have not been cited in the text.

Bibliographies

DÖRRIES, HANS, "Siedlungs-und Bevölkerungsgeographie (1908-1938)," *Geographisches Jahrbuch,* 55 (1940), 3-380. An extensive, annotated bibliography for the period indicated. Stronger in the field of settlement geography than in that of population, it is nonetheless quite useful.

OFFICE OF POPULATION RESEARCH, Princeton University, and Population Association of America, *Population Index,* quarterly, 1935- . A well-edited, comprehensive current bibliography covering all aspects of demography and peripheral fields, the starting point for any major search of the literature. Annual index to authors and places. Selected population statistics, professional news and announcements, and occasional research articles are included with the bibliographic section that comprises the bulk of this publication.

ZELINSKY, WILBUR, *A Bibliographic Guide to Population Geography.* Chicago: University of Chicago Department of Geography, Research Paper No. 80, 1962. A finding list, organized by region and topic, of all significant writings (2,588 items) published through mid-1961 that could be identified as falling within the field of population geography. A brief explanatory introduction and an author index are also provided.

In addition to the above three sources, which are specifically oriented to population, the student would do well to consult the following general geographic bibliographies: Association de Géographes Français, *Bibliographie géographique internationale,* Paris, 1892- ; American Geographical Society, *Current Geographical Publications,* New York, 1938- ; and U.S.S.R., Akademiia Nauk, Institut Nauchnoi Informatsii, *Referativnyi Zhurnal,* Moskva, 1954- .

131

Periodicals

INDIAN INSTITUTE FOR POPULATION STUDIES, *Population Review: A Journal of Asian Demography*. Madras, 1957- .

L'INSTITUT NATIONAL D'ETUDES DÉMOGRAPHIQUES, *Population*, revue trimestrielle. Paris, 1946- .

MILBANK MEMORIAL FUND, *Milbank Memorial Fund Quarterly*. New York, 1923- .

POPULATION INVESTIGATION COMMITTEE, *Population Studies. A Journal of Demography*, three times yearly. London, 1947- .

UNITED NATIONS DEPARTMENT OF SOCIAL AFFAIRS, POPULATION DIVISION, *Population Bulletin of the United Nations*, ST/SOA/Series N1- . New York, 1951- . "A recurrent publication, issued occasionally, for the presentation of studies and reports carried on for the most part, by the staff of the Population Branch of the UN."

Atlases

No adequate cartographic representation of the world's population is available as yet in book form. The following atlas is useful, but only to a limited extent. There are many valuable population maps covering limited areas or topics, published in conjunction with various monographs and articles, as well as a few wall maps and other independently issued sheet maps of distinct interest to the population geographer. Of special importance are those national atlases, such as the ones for Great Britain, Israel, Finland, Belgium, India, or Canada, that provide good coverage for the countries in question. The student in quest of such materials should use the standard bibliographic tools of the geographer if he wishes to learn what has been accomplished in the population mapping of a specific region.

BRUK, S. I., and V. S. APENCHENKO, eds. *Atlas Narodov Mira* (Atlas of the Peoples of the World). Miklukho-Maklay Institute of Ethnography, Academy of Sciences of the U.S.S.R., Moscow: Main Administration of Geodesy and Cartography (GUGK), 1964. The 106 color plates and numerous statistical tables in this unique and extremely useful Russian-language atlas show distribution of ethnic groups, languages, races, and density of population.

Statistical Compendia

UNITED NATIONS STATISTICAL OFFICE, *Demographic Yearbook*. New York, 1949- .

————, *Statistical Yearbook*. New York, 1949- .

These superbly edited annual publications not only provide a wealth of up-to-date (and some retrospective) information, but they also will lead the student to the major primary sources of official statistics. The *Demographic Yearbook* offers in each issue a series of detailed tables on selected topics, in addition to the basic tables that appear every year; and over a cycle of years statistics are offered on all topics for which useful international compilations can be made. Coverage is largely, but not entirely, limited to the national level. The *Statistical Yearbook* goes beyond the demographic field to include many social and economic items. Not listed here are the numerous statistical yearbooks, abstracts, manuals, and the like issued by virtually every nation with organized statistical services. Anyone studying a given area will need to consult the appropriate publications, not only for the data that are immediately available in them, but also for references to more detailed material.

General Studies

General introductions to demography

THOMPSON, WARREN S., *Population Problems* (4th ed.), New York: McGraw-Hill Book Company, 1953. This is, perhaps, one of the most serviceable of the general volumes on the field of demography. For additional titles, consult Eldridge's *The Materials of Demography*.

The history and methodology of population geography

JAMES, PRESTON E., "The Geographic Study of Population," in *American Geography: Inventory and Prospects,* ed. Preston E. James and Clarence F. Jones, pp. 106-22. Syracuse: Syracuse University Press, 1954. The chapter is a retrospective review of the subject.

Compendia and texts

BEAUJEU-GARNIER, JACQUELINE, *Géographie de la population.* Paris: Librairie de Médicis, 1956 and 1958. 2 vols. The closest approach to a monographic treatment of population geography yet published. The treatment is purely regional, with the quality of the individual segments varying from good to only fair. There is no attempt to examine worldwide phenomena or to extract basic principles.

GEORGE, PIERRE, *Questions de géographie de la population,* Institut National d'Etudes Démographiques, Cahiers de "Travaux et Documents," No. 34. Paris: Presses Universitaires de France, 1959. This is not a revision of George's earlier volume, but rather a completely new—and superior—work. Again, there is little regional treatment (the world is divided only into advanced and underdeveloped regions); but the chapters on distribution of numbers, fertility, mortality, and natural increase, and those on migrations and the relationships between the physical and economic environments on the one hand and population on the other, are quite illuminating.

————, *Introduction à l'étude géographique de la population du monde,* Institut National d'Etudes Démographiques, Cahiers de "Travaux et Documents," No. 14. Paris: Presses Universitaires de France, 1951. Less a general text than a broad outline (marred by Marxist tendentiousness) of the socioeconomic evolution of population, it is only the most rudimentary approach to the regionalization of population.

SPENGLER, JOSEPH J., AND OTIS DUDLEY DUNCAN, eds., *Demographic Analysis: Selected Readings.* New York: Free Press of Glencoe, Inc., 1956. A well-edited and wide-ranging collection of relatively short papers, mostly by nongeographers, but still of considerable interest to the population geographer.

TREWARTHA, GLENN T., "Population," in *Elements of Geography, Physical and Cultural* (4th ed.), pp. 501-37, V. C. Finch, G. T. Trewartha, A. H. Robinson, and E. H. Hammond. New York: McGraw-Hill Book Company, 1957. A highly concentrated, but highly rewarding, treatment of both the basic principles of the subject and the major population regions of the world.

UNITED NATIONS, *Proceedings of the World Population Conference, 1954. Rome, 31 August-10 September, 1954.* New York, 1956-57. 7 vols. Reproductions of the more than 400 papers, many of them of significance to the geographer, presented at one of the most productive meetings in the history of demography.

WITTHAUER, KURT, *Die Bevölkerung der Erde: Verteilung und Dynamik,* Ergänzungsheft Nr. 265 zu Petermanns geographischen Mitteilungen. Gotha: Haack, 1958. An impressive compendium of some basic population statistics for virtually every country of the world, along with some useful graphs and maps and brief commentaries. There is only the most elementary geographic analysis of the data.

Regional Studies

The following items are general treatments of the population of the given region, by both geographers and nongeographers, that appear especially notable to this compiler either for their factual context or as examples of excellence in the geographic or demographic analysis of population. For other general studies or for more specialized works, consult the aforementioned *A Bibliographic Guide to Population Geography,* and other bibliographic sources.

Europe

ARNBERGER, ERIK, "Grundlagen und Methoden zur kartographischen Darstellung der

Bevölkerungsentwicklung der letzten hundert Jahre in Österreich," *Osterreichischen geographischen Gesellschaft, Mitteilungen,* Vol. 102 (1960), 271-313.

KIRK, DUDLEY, *Europe's Population in the Interwar Years.* Geneva: League of Nations, 1946.

MAYER, KURT B., *The Population of Switzerland.* New York: Columbia University Press, 1952.

SMEDS, HELMER, *The Distribution of Urban and Rural Population in Southern Finland 1950,* Publicationes Instituti Geographici Universitatis Helsingiensis, No. 25, Helsinki, 1957.

U.S.S.R.

LORIMER, FRANK, *The Population of the Soviet Union: History and Prospects.* Geneva: League of Nations, 1946.

United States

BRUSH, JOHN E., *The Population of New Jersey* (2nd ed.). New Brunswick: Rutgers University Press, 1958.

BOGUE, DONALD J., *The Population of the United States.* New York: Free Press of Glencoe, Inc., 1959.

TAEUBER, CONRAD, AND IRENE B. TAEUBER, *The Changing Population of the United States.* New York: John Wiley & Sons, Inc., 1958.

UNITED STATES NATIONAL RESOURCES COMMITTEE, *The Problems of a Changing Population. Report of the Committee on Population Problems.* Washington, 1938.

VANCE, RUPERT B., *All These People: The Nation's Human Resources in the South.* Chapel Hill: University of North Carolina Press, 1945.

Latin America

LOWENTHAL, DAVID, "The Population of Barbados," *Social and Economic Studies* (Jamaica), Vol. 6 (1957), 445-501.

ROBERTS, GEORGE W., *The Population of Jamaica: An Analysis of Its Structure and Growth.* London: Cambridge University Press, 1957.

Asia

BARCLAY, GEORGE W., *Colonial Development and Population in Taiwan.* Princeton: Princeton University Press, 1954.

DAVIS, KINGSLEY, *The Population of India and Pakistan.* Princeton: Princeton University Press, 1951.

THOMPSON, WARREN S., *Population and Progress in the Far East.* Chicago: University of Chicago Press, 1959.

Africa

BARBOUR, K. M. AND R. M. PROTHERO, eds., *Essays on African Population.* London: Routledge & Kegan Paul Ltd., 1961.

BROOKFIELD, H. C., "Population Distribution in Mauritius: An Inquiry into the Determinants of Distribution in a Tropical Sugar Land," *Journal of Tropical Geography,* Vol. 13 (1959), 1-22.

FAIR, T. J. D., *The Distribution of Population in Natal,* Natal Regional Survey, Vol. 3. New York: Oxford University Press, 1955.

GILLMAN, CLEMENT, "A Population Map of Tanganyika Territory," *Geographical Review,* Vol. 26 (1936), 353-75.

GOUROU, PIERRE, *La Densité de la population au Ruanda-Urundi: Esquisse d'une étude géographique.* Institut Royal Colonial Belge, Section des Sciences Naturelles et Médicales, Mémoires, Tome 21, Fasc. 6, Bruxelles, 1953.

HILTON, THOMAS E., *Ghana Population Atlas: The Distribution and Density of Population in the Gold Coast and Togoland under United Kingdom Trusteeship.* Edinburgh: Nelson, 1960.

KUCZYNSKI, ROBERT R., *Demographic Survey of the British Colonial Empire. Vol. I. West Africa. Vol. II. East Africa, etc.* New York: Oxford University Press, 1948-49.

TREWARTHA, GLENN T., and WILBUR ZELINSKY, "The Population Geography of Belgian Africa," *Annals of the Association of American Geographers,* Vol. 44 (1954), 163-93.

NOTE: The Appendix is an abridged version of a more elaborate table prepared by the author. Copies of the original table may be obtained gratis by sending a request directly to the author.

Appendix

	1	2	3	4	5
					Population
	Population in 1,000's (Mid-1962)	Land Area (in 1,000 km^2)	Population Density (Persons/km^2)	Urban, official definition	Cities of 20,000 or more
Highly Advanced					
U.S.	186,591	9,363	20.0	69.9% ('60)	47.1% ('60)
Sweden	7,562	450	17.0	72.8 ('60)	40.8 ('60)
Canada	18,600	9,976	1.9	69.6 ('61)	39.4 ('61)
Eng. & Wales	46,768	151	309.0	80.0 ('61)	69.3 ('61)
Switzerland	5,610	41	137.0	48.3 ('60)	30.1 ('60)
W. Germany	54,766	248	221.0	71.1 ('50)	47.6 ('61)
Belgium	9,222	30	302.0	62.7 ('47)	32.0 ('47)
N. Zealand	2,485	269	9.3	64.4 ('61)	59.6 ('61)
Netherlands	11,797	34	351.0	54.6 ('47)	49.7 ('47)
Australia	10,705	7,704	1.4	78.9 ('54)	62.4 ('47)
France	47,025	551	85.0	55.9 ('54)	33.3 ('54)
Advanced					
Finland	4,505	337	13.0	55.9 ('60)	32.9 ('60)
Japan	94,930	370	256.0	63.5 ('60)	<u>72.0</u> ('60)
Argentina	21,726	2,778	7.8	62.5 ('47)	48.3 ('47)
Poland	30,324	312	98.0	48.1 ('60)	31.5 ('60)
Hungary	10,060	93	108.0	39.7 ('60)	37.4 ('60)
Spain	30,817	505	61.0	37.0 ('50)	39.8 ('50)
Transitional					
Puerto Rico	2,458	9	276.0	44.2 ('60)	28.0 ('60)
Hong Kong	3,410	1	3,366.0	76.6 ('61)	--
Chile	7,987	742	11.0	67.2 ('60)	46.3 ('60)
Mexico	37,166	1,969	19.0	50.7 ('60)	29.3 ('60)
Underdeveloped I					
Cyprus	580	9	63.0	35.9 ('60)	21.6 ('60)
Panama	1,114	75	15.0	41.5 ('60)	33.0 ('60)
Costa Rica	1,305	51	26.0	34.5 ('60)	38.0 ('63)
El Salvador	2,601	20	130.0	38.5 ('61)	--
Brazil	74,554	8,514	8.8	45.1 ('60)	28.1 ('60)
Turkey	29,059	781	37.0	31.9 ('60)	18.2 ('55)
Br. Guiana	598	215	2.8	27.6 ('46)	18.7 ('58)
Jamaica	1,641	11	144.0	23.6 ('60)	25.1 ('60)
Underdeveloped II					
Dominican Rep.	3,239	49	66.0	30.5 ('60)	--
Tunisia	4,295	125	34.0	35.6 ('56)	18.2 ('56)
Ghana	7,244	238	30.0	23.1 ('60)	11.6 ('60)
Peru	10,642	1,285	8.3	47.1 ('60)	--
Philippines	29,608	300	97.0	35.3 ('56)	--
Ceylon	10,442	66	159.0	17.6 ('56)	--
Nigeria	36,473	924	39.0	8.5 ('31)	--
Fiji Islands	421	18	230.0	18.3 ('56)	--
South Korea	26,106	98	265.0	28.0 ('60)	29.1 ('55)
Kenya	8,676	583	15.0	7.6 ('62)	--
Angola	4,950	1,247	4.0	--	4.7 ('50)
Pakistan	96,558	947	102.0	13.1 ('61)	8.0 ('51)

6 Population Cities of 100,000 or more	7 8 9 Recent Annual Change in Population			10 11 Population (1960 or 1961)		12 Crude Birth Rate (1934)
	Total	Urban	Rural	Age 0-14	65 yrs. and older	
28.5% ('60)	1.6%	2.7%	-0.01%	31.4%	9.3%	17.2
21.7 ('60)	0.6	2.2	+0.02	21.9	11.9	13.7
22.7 ('61)	2.6	4.0	-0.7	33.9	7.6	20.6
51.0 ('58)	0.5	0.5	-0.2	22.8	11.9	14.8
20.5 ('60)	1.4	2.3	+0.5	23.3	10.3	16.3
30.7 ('61)	1.2	3.2	+0.01	21.7	10.6	18.0
0.5 ('47)	0.5	0.5	-0.05	23.5	11.9	16.2
38.3 ('61)	2.3	2.3	+2.4	32.8	8.7	16.5
3.1 ('59)	1.2	1.9	+0.4	29.7	9.2	20.6
7.4 ('59)	2.3	4.5	-3.1	30.1	8.4	16.4
6.8 ('54)	1.0	1.5	+0.01	25.4	12.1	16.4
5.8 ('60)	1.0	2.8	+0.2	30.1	7.3	19.1
0.5 ('60)	0.9	8.0	-2.6	28.6 ('62)	5.9	30.0
9.5 ('58)	1.7	--	--	30.4	5.1	24.9
0.5 ('60)	1.7	3.6	+0.4	34.3	6.0	26.6
2.0 ('60)	0.7	1.5	+0.3	25.2	9.3	21.8
6.6 ('59)	0.9	--	--	27.4	8.3	26.4
3.2 ('60)	0.6	0.6	+0.6	42.7	5.2	36.9
1.0 ('56)	3.0	--	--	40.7	2.8	--
0.1 ('59)	2.5	3.7	-0.5	38.8	4.1	33.2
8.6 ('60)	3.1	4.7	+1.5	43.7	2.8	44.3
0	2.0	0	+2.2	36.9	--	30.1
5.4 ('60)	2.9	4.3	+2.0	41.5	3.9	37.1
8.0 ('63)	3.8	4.0	+3.7	44.1	2.7	43.8
9.2 ('59)	2.8	3.3	+2.4	43.1	2.6	41.5
8.7 ('61)	3.1	5.2	+1.6	42.3	2.7	--
2.1 ('60)	2.9	8.6	+0.95	41.3	3.6	--
0	2.9	3.3	+2.8	46.3	3.4	28.9
3.6 ('60)	1.3	4.3	+0.7	41.2	4.3	31.7
2.2 ('60)	3.5	5.7	+2.5	43.9	3.3	35.1
0.8 ('56)	1.9	2.0	+0.7	40.8 ('56)	--	--
7.7 ('60)	4.1	--	--	44.5	3.2	--
4.1 ('60)	2.5	3.5	+1.5	44.1	3.0	--
9.9 ('60)	3.1	4.2	+0.7	45.7	2.7	31.1
5.1 ('58)	2.9	7.5	+2.4	40.7 ('55)	1.9	37.2 ('60)
4.5 ('53)	2.0	--	--	--	--	--
--	2.0	--	--	45.1	3.3	36.8
2.8 ('59)	2.9	--	--	41.5	3.9	30.2
6.4 ('59)	3.4	--	--	--	--	--
4.3 ('55)	1.5	--	--	--	--	--
7.4 ('61)	2.1	4.6	+1.8	44.5	--	--

	13 Crude Birth Rate (1961 or 1962)	14 Reproduction Rate Gross	15 Net	16 Fertility Ratio (Children 0-4/ Women 15-44, 1960 or 1961)	17 Crude Death Rate (1934)
Highly Advanced					
U.S.	23.6	1.78 ('60)	1.72 ('60)	566	10.9
Sweden	13.7	1.06 ('60)	1.02 ('60)	343	11.2
Canada	26.9	1.87 ('61)	1.78 ('61)	606	9.5
Eng. & Wales	17.2	1.05 ('52)	1.03 ('53)	404	11.8
Switzerland	17.6	1.15 ('59)	1.09 ('59)	391	11.3
W. Germany	17.7	1.17 ('60)	1.11 ('60)	375	10.9
Belgium	16.9	1.24 ('60)	1.13 ('60)	427	12.3
N. Zealand	25.0	2.03 ('61)	1.96 ('61)	629	8.5
Netherlands	20.8	1.58 ('61)	1.52 ('61)	492	8.4
Australia	22.4	1.73 ('61)	1.66 ('61)	529	9.3
France	17.9	1.33 ('60)	1.28 ('60)	453	15.3
Advanced					
Finland	18.5	1.29 ('60)	1.22 ('60)	439	13.1
Japan	17.2	0.98 ('60)	0.92 ('60)	335	18.1
Argentina	22.3	1.4 ('61)	--	452	11.2
Poland	22.4	1.47 ('61)	1.37 ('61)	555	14.4
Hungary	14.6	0.98 ('60)	0.91 ('60)	351	14.5
Spain	21.7	1.3 ('60)	--	439	16.1
Transitional					
Puerto Rico	32.3	2.3 ('60)	--	737	18.0
Hong Kong	34.2	2.4 ('61)	--	820	28.1
Chile	36.0	2.12 ('59)	1.63 ('59)	696	26.3
Mexico	46.0	3.1 ('60)	--	787	23.8
Underdeveloped I					
Cyprus	25.3	1.7 ('53)	1.6 ('53)	617	13.2
Panama	41.0	2.80 ('61)	2.39 ('61)	752	15.7
Costa Rica	50.2	3.58 ('60)	2.84 ('60)	739	18.6
El Salvador	49.6	3.3 ('60)	--	803	25.3
Brazil	43 ('40-'45)	3.0 ('40-'45)	--	--	--
Turkey	43 ('50-'55)	2.9 ('50-'55)	--	763	--
Br. Guiana	42.9	3.0 ('60)	--	902	24.8
Jamaica	42.7	2.7 ('60)	1.86 ('55)	770	17.3
Underdeveloped II					
Dominican Rep.	44	3.2 ('50-'55)	--	798 ('50)	--
Tunisia	43.5	3.1 ('61)	--	850 ('56)	28.7 ('47)
Ghana	55.8 ('60)	3.0 ('61)	--	878	--
Peru	46	3.1 ('30-'35)	--	798	13.7
Philippines	50	3.5 ('50-'55)	--	793	16.7
Ceylon	36.6	2.5 ('60)	2.0 ('52)	761	22.9
Nigeria	53-57 ('52-'53)	3.6-3.8 ('60)	--	--	--
Fiji Islands	49.0	3.5 ('46-'51)	--	890	15.6
South Korea	45 ('50-'55)	3.1 ('50-'55)	--	659	19.6
Kenya	50 ('48)	2.9-3.4 ('48)	--	--	--
Angola	44	2.7 ('40-'45)	--	--	--
Pakistan	48 ('46-'51)	3.3 ('46-'51)	--	902	24.8*

*Applies to the whole of British India, there being no separate
statistic available for Pakistan.

18	19	20		21	22	23
Crude Death Rate '61 or '62	Repro-ductive Change Current Rate	Life Expectation at Birth (in Yrs.) Male	Female	Infant Mortality Rate (1961 or 1962)	Literates as % of Population over 15 Yrs.	GNP per Capita c. '55
9.5	14.1	67.0	73.6	25	97.8 ('59)	$ 2,343
10.1	3.6	71.2	74.9	15	99.9 ('30)	1,165
7.6	19.3	67.6 ('55-'57)	72.9	27	95.8 ('31)	1,667
11.9	5.3	68.0	73.8	21	--	998
9.8	7.8	66.4	70.8	21	--	1,229
11.1	5.6	66.7	71.9	29	--	762
12.5	4.4	62.0 ('46-'49)	67.3	28	96.7 ('47)	1,015
8.9	16.1	68.2 ('55-'57)	73.0	20	--	1,249
7.9	12.9	71.4 ('56-'60)	74.8	15	--	708
8.7	13.7	67.1 ('53-'55)	72.7	19	95.7 ('21)	1,215
11.5	6.4	67.6	74.5	26	96.6 ('46)	1,046
9.5	9.0	63.4 ('51-'55)	69.8	19	84.1 ('30)	941
7.5	9.7	65.4	70.3	29	--	240
8.0	14.3	56.9 ('47)	61.4	61	86.4 ('47)	374
7.9	14.5	64.8	70.5	56	93.8 ('50)	468
10.8	3.8	65.1 ('58)	69.4	48	95.3 ('49)	387
9.0	12.7	58.8 ('50)	63.5	42	82.4 ('50)	254
6.7	25.6	67.3	72.1	40	73.3 ('50)	511
6.0	28.2	--	--	37	44.4 ('31)	292
11.7	24.3	49.8 ('52)	53.9	116	80.4 ('52)	180
10.4	35.6	56.9	60.4	70	57.5 ('50)	187
5.9	19.4	63.6 ('48-'50)	68.8	29	60.5 ('46)	374
8.2	32.8	60.4 ('52-'54)	63.1	54	69.9 ('50)	350
8.5	41.7	54.6 ('49-'51)	57.1	72	79.4 ('50)	307
10.8	38.8	56.6	60.4	71	41.0 ('50)	244
20.6	22.4	39.3 ('40-'50)	45.5	170 ('40-'50)	49.5 ('50)	262
--	--	46.0 ('50-'51)	50.4	165	38.8 ('55)	276
8.9	34.0	49.3 ('45-'47)	52.1	51	76.0 ('46)	311
9.0	33.7	55.7 ('50-'52)	58.9	48	77.0 ('53)	265
8.4	32.6	--	--	102	66.1 ('57)	205
25.6	25.4	38.0 ('48)	--	108	--	131
15.8 ('60)	27.9	--	--	113 ('60)	--	135
8.5	37.5	--	--	97	42.4 ('40)	140
7.7	42.0	48.8 ('46-'49)	53.4 ('45-'47)	73	75.0 ('58)	201
8.6 (60)	28.0	60.3 ('54)	59.4	57 ('60)	67.7 ('53)	122
--	--	--	--	79	11.5 ('52-'53)	70
6.3	42.7	--	--	29	65.4 ('46)	--
5.3	40.0	47.2 ('38)	50.6	--	66.3 ('58)	80
--	--	--	--	--	--	61
--	--	35.0 ('40)	--	195 ('49)	3.0 ('50)	70
12.1	36.0	--	--	97 ('54)	18.9 ('51)	56

Underlining: unlikely data; quoted with reservations.
Dashes: data unavailable or completely unreliable.

Index